SHIH TZU

SMART OWNER'S GUIDE®

FROM THE EDITORS OF DOG FANCY MAGAZINE

CONTENTS

Shih Tzu, a Smart Owner's Guide®

ISBN: 978-1-593787-49-3 (Hardcover) ©2009

ISBN: 978-1-593787-47-9 (Softcover) ©2009

*photographers include Isabelle Francais; Tara Darling;
Gina Cioli and Pamela Hunnicutt. Contributing writer: Juliette Cunliffe.
Cover dog: Tango, breeder Kimberly Guinn of Aguanga, Calif. and owners Sharon
and Kathy Bilicich of Palos Verdes, Calif.*

For CIP information, see page 176.
Printed in China.

K9 EXPERT

I f you have taken a Shih Tzu into your home from a responsible breeder or a rescue group – or are planning to do so – congratulations! You have fallen in love with one of the most delightful and charming toy dog breeds.

The Shih Tzu's luxurious, long and flowing double coat is, without a doubt, the breed's claim to fame. For most owners, their first exposure to the Shih Tzu is watching a glamorous champion float around the ring at a dog show – on TV or in person. With a topknot swept up in bows and silken hair trailing the ground, the Shih Tzu's historical links to royalty come as no surprise. However, in this breed, beauty is more than skin deep. The Shih Tzu does not require a castle and a throne to be happy, nor must you maintain the floor-length coat of a show dog to enjoy the breed. Given half a chance,

The adaptable Shih Tzu has easily made the transition from the ancient Chinese imperial palaces to modern-day American penthouses.

the Shih Tzu can be all dog, doing laps around your backyard or chasing toys in your apartment, navigating an agility course, and accompanying you on shopping errands.

The American Kennel Club breed standard describes the Shih Tzu as a "sturdy, lively, alert toy dog … a highly valued, prized companion … proud of bearing … with a distinctively arrogant carriage." While the breed loves to be pampered by doting owners, Shih Tzu are nevertheless expected to be solid, substantial and well-boned. The breed standard also stipulates that as a "companion and house pet, it is essential … its temperament be outgoing, happy, affectionate, friendly and trusting towards all." So don't let the arrogant look of his upturned nose fool you: While the Shih Tzu undoubtedly possesses the stubborn streak common to all the oriental breeds, this dog is utterly devoted to his loved ones.

The breed can be high maintenance in the grooming department, but most pet owners choose to keep their dogs in a shorter puppy cut. Other owners who can't bear to lose the glorious coat that first attracted them to the breed have their groomer shave the tummy and inner legs while leaving the side coat long and flowing. It's nice to have options.

Not only does the Shih Tzu allow for variety in coat length and style but in color as well. The parti-colors – white with black, gold, silver or chocolate markings – are the most popular and very dramatic, but the breed also comes in a rainbow of solid shades, from deep black, rich red and charcoal gray to pale silver and gold.

JOIN OUR ONLINE Club Shih Tzu®

With this Smart Owner's Guide®, you are well on your way to getting your toy dog diploma. But your Shih Tzu education doesn't end here. You're invited to join **Club Shih Tzu®** (**DogChannel.com/Club-ShihTzu**), a FREE online site with lots of fun and instructive features like:

◆ **forums, blogs** and **profiles** to connect with other Shih Tzu owners
◆ **downloadable charts** and **checklists** to help you be a smart and loving Shih Tzu owner
◆ access to Shih Tzu **e-cards** and **screensavers**
◆ interactive **games**
◆ canine **quizzes**

The **Smart Owner's Guide®** series and **Club Shih Tzu®** are backed by the experts at DOG FANCY® magazine and DogChannel.com, who have been providing trusted and up-to-date information about dogs and dog lovers for more than 40 years. Log on and join the club today!

Whatever your plans for this new addition – show dog, obedience star or thoroughly spoiled pet – you and your Shih Tzu will quickly form a loving bond. Soon, you'll be asking yourself the same question that other Shih Tzu owners the world over have: How did I manage so long without one?

Allan Reznik
Editor-at-Large, DOG FANCY

A DIVA?!

Many people take great pride in the jobs their dogs were meant to do. A Golden Retriever who brings back a fallen bird or a Border Collie who controls sheep are invaluable to the hunter and shepherd who work with them. Countless other dogs tap into their breed's history by pointing, flushing, herding or retrieving in competition, much to the delight of their enthusiastic owners.

All too often, these same owners see the tiny Shih Tzu and refer to him as "just a toy dog" or "only a lap dog." How wrong they are. True, this distinctive dog was developed with a single purpose in mind, but what a purpose: to be a companion! In a society that emphasizes entertainment and meaningful, happy relationships, it is only natural that the Shih Tzu walks with his head held high!

Anyone who has the privilege of sharing his or her life with these entertaining and exuberant dogs knows they take their jobs just as seriously as other dogs take theirs. The Shih Tzu knows that being a good companion dog requires versatility, dedication and constant affection, and he fulfills his job requirements with unparalleled ease.

it's a Fact

If you don't want a dog with long locks of hair that need constant upkeep, you can still welcome a Shih Tzu into your home. Her coat can be kept in a puppy cut, which is relatively short and easy to maintain.

THE STANDARD SAYS ...

The Shih Tzu is described as a small, intelligent and extremely docile dog in the breed standard, a written description by the national breed club of what an ideal Shih Tzu should look and act like. It is truly a companion dog who likes to be near his master. Since the sole purpose of the breed is that of a companion and house pet, the ideal Shih Tzu temperament is outgoing, happy, affectionate, friendly and trusting.

The breed standard also states: "The Shih Tzu is a sturdy, lively, alert toy dog with a long, flowing double coat. Befitting his noble Chinese ancestry as a highly valued, prized companion and palace pet, the Shih Tzu is proud of bearing, has a distinctively arrogant carriage with head well up and tail curved over the back ..."

How do these traits translate in the home setting? What is it like to live with this energetic and enchanting but stubborn little dog? These answers and more lie within the pages of this book.

CHARACTER TRAITS

Shih Tzu are strictly indoor dogs, not yard dogs. Simply put: They don't thrive in a situation where they are separated from their people. If they are indoors, though, they have to be protected from becoming overheated. They can tolerate cold much better than heat. The shape of a Shih Tzu face makes it a little difficult for him to breathe. Your Shih Tzu should never be put in a situation where he doesn't have access to open air.

Because of their pride and stubbornness, the Shih Tzu is not easy to train. After all, in ancient times, all the Shih Tzu had to do was strike a pose and look beautiful. This attitude seems to have persisted through the centuries. It can be challeng-

ing for owners to make their Shih Tzu believe what he really wants to do is what his owner asks of him.

Shih Tzu don't like rules. They have relatively short attention spans and selectively short memories. They get distracted and forget where they are and what rules apply.

If you're looking for an easy-to-train dog, a Shih Tzu isn't for you. Shih Tzu's train you!

These are traits that make them the happy-go-lucky clowns who attract people in the first place, so be patient during training sessions. When you first introduce a new concept, your Shih Tzu is likely to go along with the idea just to amuse you. After all, that is his life's purpose.

HOUSETRAINING HORRORS?

Getting the concept of housetraining across to a Shih Tzu will present the greatest challenge to even the smartest and most patient owner. It is probably easier to train him to use a newspaper or pad than it is to teach him to go outside. Waiting is not in the Shih Tzu's nature. Sometimes, they will choose to forget their training if you have done something they don't approve of.

If your Shih Tzu still has a lot of puppy hair, or if his coat is trim with full hair on the legs, it might be more of a challenge to housetrain him. Remember, these are small dogs. They have short legs and are close to the ground, which makes it very difficult to see if they are squatting or lifting a leg. Lots of mistakes may be made along the road to housetraining success, but your patience will eventually pay off. Plan ahead to spend the time needed to get the message across. If you are right there when the task is done, lots of praise and a few treats will get your dog's attention, and with any luck your vision of a housetrained Shih Tzu will come to fruition. It is also possible to train a small dog such as the Shih Tzu to use a litter box for potty emergencies.

DON'T LEAVE ME!

Shih Tzu have a difficult time being alone. They are people dogs and want to be with their family as much as possible, if not all the time.

Life isn't perfect for any of us, though, and there are times when your Shih Tzu must be by himself. Under those circumstances, he will need a comforting place of his own. A comfy bed is good, but a crate is better. If you have your puppy spend time in his crate when you first bring him home, he will quickly learn that his crate is his very own safe haven.

Quite often, if you leave the crate door open, when your dog is tired of amusing you, he will voluntarily go into his crate to rest. If you make the crate an attractive place — a soft cushion, water bottle and a few toys — it becomes a little get-

Shih Tzu were bred to be companion dogs, so they need owners who enjoy affectionate toy dogs.

away suite for your Shih Tzu. Once he is accustomed to spending time in his crate, your Shih Tzu will be happier if he has to go to the vet, to the kennel or on an airplane. No matter the situation, your Shih Tzu will feel comfortable and safe in his crate.

WON'T LIFT A PAW

No matter how you spell it, "work" is not something a Shih Tzu likes to do; they weren't bred to work. Instead, they were bred to charm and amuse their owners and produce even more glorious offspring. Expecting a Shih Tzu to perform formal obedience work is almost an insult. They will do some exercises one day, all of them the next day and none of them the following day. They often wait until an obedience trial to do something entirely incorrect, thereby completely embarrassing you but amusing the spectators. And if the spectators laugh, you can be sure your Shih Tzu will enter that trick into his repertoire to save for another dull day that needs a bit of lightheartedness.

OWNER'S TRAITS

To live with, and truly appreciate, a Shih Tzu, there are some things smart owners need to keep in mind:

Flexibility: When you're owned by a Shih Tzu (yes, you read that right!), be patient and willing to compromise on a daily basis. You may have rules and your dog might allow you to think he is following them, but that will only happen if there is a payoff for your dog. You can't rely on your Shih Tzu's behavior to be consistent. It all depends on how much your dog wants his payoff.

Firm Kindness: Being an ancient breed, Shih Tzu tend to think they know it all, but there will be times when your dog will have to compromise too. A smart owner will ask

For a long time, we thought of Shih Tzu as dogs who should be on a pillow or in the house, but we're finding that they love to do agility and obedience. We now have both obedience and agility at our national specialty, and the number of entries is growing each year. Many Shih Tzu owners are finishing their dogs in conformation and then working on another title, proving these dogs do have brains and love doing things with their owners.

— Carlene Snyder, a Shih Tzu breeder from Brandon, Fla.

Did You Know?

From birth until about 2 weeks, the newborn puppy is in the neonatal period. She's blind and deaf, but her other senses work just fine. Some experts recommend that a breeder stimulate those senses by gradually subjecting these puppies not only to being physically handled and petted, but also to mildly stressful events, such as briefly elevating the little one by placing her on a table.

their dog to follow a cue and will be consistent in enforcing that cue.

Good Sense of Humor: Unless yours is a strange Shih Tzu, he will be the family clown. Sometimes this backfires and what your dog thought might be amusing doesn't go over very well with you, but those times tend to be fairly rare.

It takes time to develop a true appreciation for your Shih Tzu's entertaining talents. It's easier if your dog has been in your household since puppyhood because the both of you can grow together and mutually establish rules. If the Shih Tzu comes into your home as an older puppy or an adult, he will sit back and take time to observe his new family to see what your humor level might be and where he might refine it to fit in perfectly.

JOIN OUR ONLINE Club Shih Tzu®

Show your artistic side. Share photos, videos and artwork of your favorite breed on Club Shih Tzu You can also submit jokes, riddles and even poetry about Shih Tzu. Browse through our various galleries and see the talent of fellow toy dog owners. Go to **DogChannel.com/Club-ShihTzu** and click on "Galleries" to get started.

I find that their wonderful temperaments make Shih Tzu ideal household pets and companions;. their size is perfect for an apartment or home. No one can resist the charm and appeal of a Shih Tzu puppy with those big black eyes and furry little bodies.

— Victor Joris, Shih Tzu expert, dog show judge and author

True to their imperial heritage, Shih Tzu remain a part of the high life. In a *New York Times* article dated Oct. 24, 2003, it was reported that more Shih Tzu (160 at the time) lived on the Upper East Side — the posh 10021 area code — than in any other neighborhood in the city.

Older Than Three: The Shih Tzu should never be expected to be a plaything for a child who cannot even walk. Children have to be trained and taught how to hold, and deal with, a Shih Tzu and how not to. If a child hits your Shih Tzu; pulls on his ears, tail or hair; steps on or drops him, your dog may be traumatized forever. If you are expecting young children to visit your home, it would be best to leave your dog in his crate for his own protection.

Younger Than 100: This is really a hard one. Older people tend to want a lap dog and that's OK; but keep in mind, Shih Tzu are active and bouncy and like to run around right beside, behind or in front of their owner's feet. This spells trouble for an older person who might use walker. The last thing you want is to trip and injure a person.

Experience with Dogs: A Shih Tzu's dream is to be in a home with an owner who is experienced with dogs, particularly small toy dogs.

A Shih Tzu–experienced owner has the best traits and will be more aware of the special care and needs of the Shih Tzu.

Special Needs: Many Shih Tzu have problems with eye discharge. They can see just fine, but their eyes tend to run a lot due to problematic tear ducts. When there is hair all over their face, the tears get stuck and can start to smell. No Shih Tzu owner wants to play kissy with a smelly face, and Shih Tzu do like to kiss! To maintain this jovial relationship, your Shih Tzu needs to have his face gently washed with warm water daily. If the eye discharge is excessive, a trip to the vet is in order since there may be a simple medical remedy.

Brushing your Shih Tzu is necessary, especially because your Shih Tzu has longer hair on his ears and legs. If you give your Shih Tzu a puppy cut, he is less likely to get mats and unsightly tangles in his coat. The optimal grooming regimen would involve regular trips to the groomer. Baths and massages feel so good to him, and when a Shih Tzu is looking his best, he definitely gives the Poodle a run for his money for "most glamorous dog."

Despite their proud and dignified countenance, Shih Tzu are quite clownish and love to make their owners laugh.

Shih Tzu are masters of deception!

While you're busy training your Shih Tzu, you're little dog is busy training you!

All dogs direct or train their people to some extent, but the Shih Tzu elevates such owner training to an art. Just ask Jo Ann White, former president of the American Shih Tzu Club.

White recalls that one of her own Shih Tzu, Duke, didn't have any trouble training White's late husband to give him a treat. But Duke — a champion show dog whose formal name was Heavenly Dynasty's Regal Duke — didn't just demand a treat; instead, he took a more *subtle* approach to teaching his master to give him what he wanted.

"If Duke wanted a cookie, he would first sneeze, then whimper, then paw at my husband's leg," recalls White, who resides in Bradenton, Fla. "Then, he would yodel louder and louder until my husband finally gave him a cookie so he could hear the television again."

According to White, Duke's training talent epitomizes the Shih Tzu temperament.

"Duke's people-training is typical of the breed," she says. "It's all in how you deal with it, and you have to be careful not to let Shih Tzu charm you into allowing them to become spoiled. The cookie trick always worked with my husband, but Duke never tried it on me because he knew I wouldn't respond. So it wasn't worth the effort."

Duke trained White's husband to dispense treats on canine command as well as limit his arguments with his wife.

"My husband and I could never argue for long because the Shih Tzu would whimper and paw at my husband's leg if he raised his voice," White says.

White's experiences with Duke and countless other Shih Tzu have led her to conclude that "people who say Shih Tzu train you, rather than the other way around, are definitely correct."

Shih Tzu may be pampered divas, but they are very generous with their love and affection.

A SHIH TZU SUMMARY

High energy, friendly and trusting make this small dog the perfect companion.

COUNTRY OF ORIGIN: Tibet/China

WHAT HIS FRIENDS CALL HIM: Fo Dog, Chrysanthemum-faced Dog, Powder Puff

SIZE: 8 to 11 inches tall at the shoulders; 9 to 16 pounds

COAT & COLOR: The Shih Tzu's luxurious, dense, long and flowing double coat comes in all colors and combinations.

PERSONALITY TRAITS: Shih Tzu are happy and outgoing, with a friendly, trusting attitude. Bred to be companion dogs, they are lively, alert and affectionate.

WITH KIDS: These dogs are good with children who have been taught to handle them carefully.

WITH OTHER PETS: Shih Tzu are good with other animals — just as long as they remain the center of attention.

ENERGY LEVEL: high

EXERCISE NEEDS: Daily walks are a necessity.

GROOMING NEEDS: Shih Tzu require brushing at least twice a week, but sometimes more; they also need weekly baths. Be sure to keep the face washed, the hair out of their eyes, the nails trimmed and the ears cleaned. A professional groomer can maintain a Shih Tzu with one of several convenient clips.

TRAINING NEEDS: These dogs enjoy short training sessions but may require a few tries before they master a new technique.

LIVING ENVIRONMENT: Shih Tzu make an excellent pet for apartment dwellers.

LIFESPAN: 12 to 14 years

The Shih Tzu is known as "little lion" or "lion dog" in his adopted land of China, though he probably originated in the mountainous country of Tibet. Stately and powerful, lions have long been a symbol of royalty, even in cultures such as Tibet and China, where lions were not indigenous.

The lion also holds a special place in Buddhist mythology: They were guards of Buddha's throne. In his 1927 book *Dogs: Their History and Development*, canine historian Edward C. Ash wrote that the Buddha lions "were produced by stretching forward his hand, his fingers changing into five lions, which — roaring with a voice that shook the heavens — brought enemies into subjection."

Because real lions were unsuited to the Asian climate — as well as inconvenient and dangerous to keep — Tibetan lamas (the country's spiritual leaders), and later, the imperial Chinese kennels, bred small dogs meant to resemble the lion. Early depictions of these canine "lions" can be only described as fantastical. It's unclear whether the lion dogs were drawn to resemble symbolic lions

Did You Know? The American Kennel Club breed standard states that a Shih Tzu's weight should be between 9 and 16 pounds. There are no such things as "teacup" or "imperial" Shih Tzu; a reputable breeder will not use these terms.

or if the artists and sculptors exaggerated the features to make them seem more lion-like.

MINGLING WITH GREATNESS

We don't know exactly when the Shih Tzu first became a distinct breed. As with so many breeds, the passage of centuries has drawn a veil across the Shih Tzu's original face. Advances in genetic testing, however, tell us that this breed is one of the most ancient breeds in existence, along with other dogs of Asian origin including the Chow Chow, Shar-Pei, Pekingese and Tibetan Terrier.

However he came to be, the lion dog became a part of life in Tibetan monasteries, where the lamas lived. These lamaseries were famed as the promulgators of shaggy dogs, all known as *apsos*, which best translates to "goat-like" or "bearded," likely a reference to their coats. The largest of these were mastiff-type dogs, who served as fierce guardians of the royal palaces. The medium-sized dogs, known today as Tibetan Terriers, were nicknamed "luck bringers" and often traveled high plateaus with nomadic herdsmen to guard their tents. The smallest were bred to be companions and watchdogs, qualities that have characterized them

it's a Fact

The chrysanthemum, described in Chinese writings as early as 1400 B.C., was highly valued as an herb and as a flower. It was believed to possess the power of life. "If you would be happy for a lifetime, grow chrysanthemums," advised one Chinese sage. The Shih Tzu came to be known as the chrysanthemum-faced dog because the hair on her face grew in all directions like the petals of the cherished flower.

Toy dogs like toys. Be sure to keep your Shih Tzu occupied with plenty of fun and interesting toys.

Talk about being a diva: The Shih Tzu's lineage can be traced to the royal palaces of imperial China.

through the centuries and into the present day. All of these dogs had two things in common: a heavy coat to protect them during Tibet's frigid winters and a tail that curved up and over the back.

Known for being happy and entertaining, the smallest apsos were the subject of a number of legends. One legend regarded them as incarnations of mischievous household gods; another, that they contained the souls of lamas who had not yet reached nirvana, the attainment of wisdom and the transcendence of the desires of this life. These small apsos later made their way west as gifts to diplomats and other important personages, and became today's Shih Tzu: the non-sporting, slightly larger and more aloof version of the Lhasa Apso.

From Tibet, the Shih Tzu may have traveled in caravans to the Chinese empire, as a gift from Tibet to the emperor. This gift reflected the emperor's high status as well as the regard in which the lion dog was held. After all, only the best could be given to such a mighty ruler.

When the first gift of apsos was made is unknown; theories suggest that it may have been as early as the T'ang Dynasty (A.D. 618 to 907), a period during which China was exposed to many other cultures. Documents, paintings and other artifacts indicate that dogs similar to the Shih Tzu have been tracked since at least A.D. 624.

Shih Tzu scholars believe the breed could have arrived in China during the T'ang Dynasty as a gift from K'iu T'ai, king of Viqur, who may have acquired them from somewhere in the vast Byzantine Empire. Lion dogs were again mentioned some time between A.D. 990 and 994, as tribute from the people of Ho Chou. Because all of this occurred more than 1,000 years ago, much of this breed's history is based on hearsay or may have been lost in translation, so not much is known for sure. Lack or loss of records, invasions and other disasters have contributed to the breed's lost history. Yet, another theory suggests that these dogs did not reach China until some time between 1850 and 1908, as a gift from a Dalai Lama. What we do know is that in China, the dogs who became known as the Shih Tzu were probably bred with other small imperial dogs, most likely Pekingese and possibly Pugs, to achieve a more stylized appearance.

**You have an unbreakable bond with your dog, but do you
always understand her?** Go online and download "Dog Speak,"
which outlines how dogs communicate. Find out what your
Shih Tzu is saying when she barks, howls or growls. Go to
DogChannel.com/Club-ShihTzu and click on "Downloads."

SMART TIP!

Shih Tzu litters range from one to eight puppies, but the average litter size is around three to five. Pups are ready to go to their new homes at about 12 weeks of age. Before you consider the characteristics of the puppy you want — color, sex, temperament — consider whether or not your home and lifestyle are right for this breed.

The "recipe" for the breed's creation, as fancifully described by James Mumford in an issue of the *American Shih Tzu Magazine* is: "a dash of lion, several teaspoons of rabbit, a couple ounces of domestic cat, one part court jester, a dash of ballerina, a pinch of old man (Chinese), a bit of beggar, a tablespoon of monkey, one part baby seal, a dash of teddy bear and the rest of the dogs of Tibetan and Chinese origin."

THE LION KING

From China's Ming Dynasty (1368–1644) — a time of brilliance in literature, art and thought — through the Qing Dynasty (1644–1911), the Shih Tzu is said to have been a popular member of the imperial household. Their breeding was overseen by eunuchs in the Forbidden City in Peking (today's Beijing), although unfortunately, records of breedings were not kept or were lost in the flames of the 1911 Xinhai Revolution.

Toward the end of the Qing Dynasty, the empress took an interest in Shih Tzu breeding. T'zu Hsi was the dowager empress of China and a very powerful woman.

Shih Tzu and Lhasa Apso are somewhat similar in appearance to a novice. Be sure to find a reputable breeder, or you could end up with a non-pure mix.

Is the Shih Tzu the Right Dog for You?

"To truly tell if a Shih Tzu is the right breed for someone, that person needs to spend time with a few Shih Tzu," says David Ritchkoff, a breeder in Boston, Mass., member of the American Shih Tzu Club and former vice president of the Puritan Shih Tzu Club. "Find a nearby breeder, and visit at least once to determine if the Shih Tzu feels like the correct breed for your lifestyle. I also recommend reading books on the breed to help flesh out any other information you might need."

An affectionate breed, Shih Tzu thrive on human contact. If your lifestyle doesn't allow for spending considerable time with your dog, consider another type of pet.

"A Shih Tzu is a full-time responsibility," says Kerrie Butterfield, a Shih Tzu owner from Spokane, Wash. "My pup goes everywhere possible with me. He sleeps in bed with me, and many times takes over my pillow. He also loves to be on my lap, desk and feet — wherever I am. Shih Tzu are very loyal, loving dogs and I have yet to find another breed that is so affectionate and trusting. Shih Tzu are also very smart, and they learn very quickly. They love to be spoiled!"

If you decide that you want a Shih Tzu, you may have to wait a while to locate your perfect Shih Tzu pup.

"Most quality Shih Tzu breeders in the United States are actually very small operations that do not have many litters a year," Ritchkoff warns. "Shih Tzu puppies are not merchandise that can be immediately plucked off a shelf when someone wants one. Good things are definitely worth waiting for when it comes to purebred dogs. Usually, people can expect a wait of at least a few months for a puppy from a quality breeder."

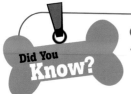

She lived from 1835 to 1908, and when she wasn't ruling China, she was busy supervising the imperial kennels, which contained Shih Tzu, Pekingese and Pugs. One photograph of T'zu Hsi shows her with a black Shih Tzu who is said to have followed her as she made her daily rounds through the palace. After the empress' death, imperial rule in China began to crumble and the breeding of palace dogs fell by the wayside.

Fortunately, Shih Tzu ownership was not limited to the imperial household. Some may have been given as gifts or perhaps secretly sold by the eunuchs to Chinese nobility. Eventually, they fell into the hands of foreigners, the most well-known of them being General Douglas and Lady Brownrigg. On a trip to Hong Kong, they reportedly saw a Shih Tzu and fell in love. By 1930, Shih Tzu had made their way to England, saving the breed from what probably would have been extinction during the struggle to establish China as a republic. According to the American Kennel Club's history of the breed, every Shih Tzu today can be traced to only 14 dogs: seven females and seven males.

The two black and white Shih Tzu that came to England with the Brownriggs were a male named Hibou and a female named Shu-ssa, according to England's Shih Tzu Club. Shu-ssa was exhibited at the renowned Crufts Dog Show in 1936 and was named Best of Breed. She was described as having a thick but smooth coat that stuck out on her head and face, giving her the appearance of a baby owl or, appropriately for the breed, a chrysanthemum blossom. The Brownriggs called their kennel Taishan and bred Shu-ssa to Hibou, as well as to a dog named Lung-fu-ssa, owned by Madelaine Hutchins of Ireland. Shu-ssa's puppies were the progenitors of many of today's Shih Tzu. Other contributors to the breed's start in England are attributed to Hutchins and Madame de Breuil, a Russian refugee.

WORLDWIDE RECOGNITION

Despite their survival in England, there were a few bumps in the road to the breed's development. In England, the Shih Tzu was originally called a Tibetan Lion Dog and classified as an apso, placing him in the same category as his cousin from Tibet, the Lhasa Apso. Some Shih Tzu were even registered with the AKC as Lhasa Apsos, and two of them sometimes still show up in Lhasa pedigrees that go back far enough. The two breeds were quite different in appearance, however, a fact that became obvious when the two were shown together in 1933 at the West of England Ladies

JOIN OUR ONLINE Club Shih Tzu®

Just how quickly will your Shih Tzu puppy grow? Go to Club Shih Tzu and download a growth chart. You can also track your pup's age in human years; the old standard of multiplying your dog's age by seven isn't quite accurate. Log onto **DogChannel.com/Club-ShihTzu** and click on "Downloads."

Shih Tzu are extremely smart little dogs. They learn how to deal with their owners quickly; they learn how to bend their humans around their paws, so to speak. If you allow them to, they'll run the house. They decide what goes on.

— breeder Nancy Beeman of Dayton, Ohio, who also trains and shows Shih Tzu

Kennel Society Championship show. One main difference, according to England's Shih Tzu Club, was that the Lhasa Apso has a narrower skull and longer nose.

The dual classification concerned Lhasa Apso breeders, who feared that the two breeds would be confused. England's Kennel Club ruled that they were indeed separate breeds and required that the apso be renamed. It was christened the Shih Tzu, and in 1935, the breed club, which had been The Apso and Lion Dog Club, became the Shih Tzu Club.

The club then took on the task of standardizing the Shih Tzu. With the assistance of the Brownriggs, the club wrote a breed standard and carefully recorded and inspected litters to ensure that all Shih Tzu registered met the breed standard. By 1939, more than 100 Shih Tzu were registered.

The breed's development slowed somewhat during World War II, but the Shih Tzu managed to survive, although many dogs did not. In fact, the Taishan Shih Tzu even contributed to the war effort. Lady Brownrigg collected their fur when they were combed and turned it into wool for knitting.

In 1947, two years after the war's end, two Shih Tzu owned by Lady Brownrigg earned championships, becoming the first two Shih Tzu to do so. They were Ch. Ta Chi of Taishan and Ch. Yo Mo of Chunang of Boydon.

The 1950s and '60s were a high point of the breed's development in England, although this golden age, as it has been described, began with a scandal. In 1952, Pekingese breeder Freda Evans of Elfann Kennels acquired two Shih Tzu and crossed them with Pekingese, believing it would improve the Shih Tzu breed. The Shih Tzu was often criticized for being too big and leggy and having too long of a nose. This was done without the approval of the Kennel Club, and it was not until four generations later that the Kennel Club accepted descendants of these dogs as purebred Shih Tzu. Today, if a pedigree is researched far enough, many Shih Tzu in Britain have the Elfann Pekingese in their family tree.

Given their charm, attractive appearance and romantic history, it's no surprise that Shih Tzu quickly became popular and spread throughout the world. They were exported to other countries in Europe, as well as to Australia. According to the AKC, American soldiers stationed abroad during World War II discovered the Shih Tzu and brought them home with them in the 1940s. The Shih Tzu is one of the youngest of the AKC-recognized breeds, having been admitted to the stud book in 1969. They were, of course, classified as a toy breed. Today, the Shih Tzu is one of the most popular breeds registered by the AKC.

Did You Know?

When it wrote the breed standard for the Shih Tzu, The Peking Kennel Club also broke into fits of prose. It described the breed as having "the head of a lion, the round face of an owl, the lustrous eyes of a dragon, the oval tongue of a peony petal, the mouth of a frog, teeth like grains of rice, ears like palm leaves, the torso of a bear, the broad back of a tiger, the tail of a Phoenix, the legs of an elephant, toes like a mountain range, a yellow coat like a camel and the movement of a fish."

Though the Shih Tzu has been around for centuries, it wasn't until 1969 that it was officially recognized by the American Kennel Club.

SELECTION

Once you've done a bit of research and have decided you'd like to be the proud owner of an adorable Shih Tzu, your next step should be to select a reputable breeder. However, in today's age of information, it's sometimes difficult to know where to look and who to trust.

Well, don't worry! We'll show you the best places to find a responsible and ethical breeder, and help you prepare a list of questions you should ask a breeder during the interview process, as well as fill you in on what the breeder will want to know about you and your household.

INVEST IN A GOOD BREEDER

You're going to have your Shih Tzu for 12 to 14 years, so the time to find a healthy, well-adjusted pup from a reputable breeder will pay off for you in the long run. Look for a breeder who values good health and stable personalities, and one who really cares about what happens to your dog for the rest of his life spent with you.

it's a **Fact**

Have your pup examined by a veterinarian within two to three days after bringing her home. If declared unhealthy, the breeder should take your dog back without any problems. This shows the breeder's confidence and that he stands behind his dogs. The willingness to rehome a puppy is the ultimate hallmark of a good breeder.

Be sure to avoid puppy mills and backyard breeders. Puppy mills are large-scale breeding operations that produce puppies in an assembly-line fashion without regard to health and socialization. Backyard breeders are typically well-meaning, regular pet owners who simply do not possess enough knowledge about their breed and breeding to produce healthy puppies.

The American Kennel Club (www.akc.org) and United Kennel Club (www.ukcdogs.com) provide lists of breeders in good standing with their organization. Visit their website for more information.

EVALUATING BREEDERS

Once you have the names and numbers of breeders in your area, start contacting them to find out more about their breeding programs. But, before you pick up the phone, plan to ask the questions that will get you the information you need to know.

Prospective buyers should interview breeders much the same way that a breeder interviews a buyer. Make a list of questions and record the answers so you can compare them to the answers from other breeders whom you may interview later. The right questions are those that help you identify who has been in the breed a respectable number of years and who is actively showing their dogs. Ask in-depth questions regarding the genetic health of the parents, grandparents and great-grandparents of any puppy you are considering. Be sure to ask what sort of genetic testing program the breeder adheres to.

A prospective buyer should look to see if a breeder actively shows his or her dogs. Showing indicates that the breeder is bringing out examples from his or her breeding program for the public to see. If there are any obvious problems, such as temperament or general conformation, they will be obvious. Also, the main reason to breed dogs is to improve the quality of the breed. If the breeder is not showing, then he or she is more likely breeding purely for monetary reasons and may have less concern for the welfare and future of the breed.

Smart potential puppy buyers inquire about health, and determine the breeder's willingness to work with them in the future. The prospective buyer should see what kind of health guarantees the breeder gives. You should also find out if the breeder will be available for future consultation regarding your dog, and find out if the breeder will take your dog back if something unforeseen happens.

Prospective buyers should ask plenty of questions, and in return, buyers should also be prepared to answer questions posed by a responsible breeder who wants to make sure their Shih Tzu puppy is going to a good home. Be prepared for a battery of questions from the breeder regarding your purpose for wanting a Shih Tzu and whether or not you can properly care for one. Avoid buying from a breeder who does little or no screening. If breeders don't ask questions, they are not concerned with where their puppies end up. In this case, the Shih Tzu's best interests are probably not the breeder's motive for breeding. You should find a breeder who is willing

Did You Know?

Good Breeder Indicators
When you visit a Shih Tzu breeder, be sure to look around the location for:
- a clean, well-maintained facility
- no overwhelming odors
- overall impression of cleanliness
- socialized dogs and puppies

NOTABLE & QUOTABLE

Find out why the breeder breeds his or her dogs, what health issues the breed has and whether they offer health and genetic guarantees. Ask questions and get specific answers regarding vaccine regiments, deworming, potty schedules and where the puppies are raised and socialized.

— Tressa West, a Shih Tzu breeder in Cookeville, Tenn.

to answer any questions you have and is knowledgeable about the history of the breed, health issues and about the background of their own dogs. Learn about a breeder's long-term commitment to the breed and to their puppies after they leave the kennel.

Look for a breeder who knows their purpose for producing a particular litter, one that is knowledgeable of their dogs' pedigrees and of the breed itself, and has had the necessary health screenings performed on the parents. The breeder should also be asking you for references if they are interested in establishing a relationship with you. If after one phone conversation with a breeder, the person is supplying you with an address to send a deposit, continue your search for a reputable breeder elsewhere.

CHOOSING THE RIGHT PUP

Once you have found a breeder you are comfortable with, your next step is to pick the right puppy for you. The good news is that if you have done your homework in finding a responsible breeder, you can count on this person to give you plenty of help in choosing the right pup for your personality and lifestyle. In fact, most good

breeders will recommend a specific puppy to a buyer once they know what kind of dog the buyer is seeking.

After you have narrowed down the search and selected a reputable breeder, rely on the experience of the breeder to help you select the perfect puppy for you. The selection of the puppy depends a lot on what purpose the pup is being purchased for. If the pup is being purchased as a show prospect, the breeder will offer their assessment of the pups who meet this criteria and be able to explain the strengths and faults of each pup.

Whether your pup is show- or pet-quality, a good, stable temperament is vital for a happy relationship. Generally, you want to avoid a timid puppy or one who is very dominant. Temperament is very important, and a reputable breeder should spend a lot of time with the pups and be able to offer an evaluation of each pup's personality.

Reputable breeders should tell each buyer which puppy is appropriate for his or her home situation and personality. They may not allow you to choose the puppy, although they will certainly take your preference into consideration.

Some breeders, on the other hand, believe it's important for you to have a strong involvement in picking a puppy from the litter. Not everyone is looking for the same things in a dog. Some people want a quiet, laidback attitude; others want an outgoing and active dog.

When pups are old enough to go to their new homes at roughly 12 weeks of age, some breeders prefer you make your own decision because no one can tell at this age which pup will make the most intelligent or affectionate dog who will fit in your home. The color, sex and markings are obvious, but that is about all you can tell for sure at this age. Everything else being equal — size, health,

Did You Know?

A healthy puppy has clear eyes, a shiny coat, and is playful and friendly. An important factor in a puppy's long-term health and good temperament is the age she goes to his permanent home, which should be at about 12 weeks. This gives the pup plenty of time to develop immunity and bond with her mother.

Finding the perfect Shih Tzu pup starts with finding a reputable breeder who always has his or her Shih Tzu's best interest in mind.

Questions to Expect
Be prepared for the breeder to ask you some questions, too.

1. Have you previously owned a Shih Tzu?

The breeder is trying to gauge how familiar you are with the breed. If you have never owned one, illustrate your knowledge of Shih Tzu by telling the breeder about your research.

2. Do you have children? What are their ages?

Some breeders are wary about selling a toy dog to families with younger children. This isn't a steadfast rule, and some breeders only insist on meeting the children to see how they handle puppies. It all depends on the breeder.

3. How long have you wanted a Shih Tzu?

This helps a breeder know if this purchase is an impulse buy, or a carefully thought-out decision. Buying on impulse is one of the biggest mistakes owners can make. Be patient.

Join Club Shih Tzu to get a complete list of questions a breeder should ask you. Click on "Downloads" at: **DogChannel.com/Club-ShihTzu**

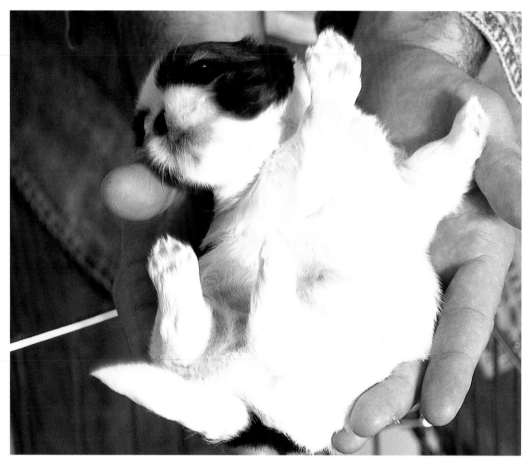

etc. — you might just pick the pup you have a gut feeling for.

Chemistry between buyer and puppy is important and should play a role in determining which pup goes to which home. When possible, make numerous visits, and in effect, let a puppy choose you. There will usually be one puppy who spends more time with a buyer and is more comfortable relaxing and sitting with or on a person.

CHECKING FOR SHIH TZU QUALITIES

Whether you are dealing with a breeder who wants to pick a pup for you or lets you make the decision, consider certain points when evaluating the pup you may end up calling your own. The pup should be friendly and outgoing, not skittish in any way. He should be forgiving of correction. He shouldn't be too terribly mouthy. The pup should readily follow you, be willing to snuggle in your lap and be turned onto his back easily without a problem.

Proper temperament is important. A Shih Tzu puppy who has a dominant personality requires an experienced owner who will be firm during training. A puppy who is a little shy requires heavy socialization to build his confidence.

With the breeder's permission, evaluate each puppy's temperament on your own. The temperament of the pups can be evaluated by spending some time watching them. If you can visit the pups and observe them

With the popularity of Shih Tzu, shelters and rescue groups across the country are often inundated with sweet, loving examples of the breed — from the tiniest puppies to senior dogs.

Finding the Shih Tzu of your dreams, only takes a journey to the local animal shelter. Or, perhaps you could find your ideal dog waiting patiently in the arms of a foster parent at a nearby rescue group. It just takes a bit of effort, patience and a willingness to find the right dog for your family — not just the cutest dog on the block.

The perks of owning a Shih Tzu are plentiful: companionship, unconditional love, true loyalty and laughter, just to name a few. So why choose the adoption option? Because you literally will be saving a life!

Owners of adopted dogs swear they're more grateful and loving than any dog they've owned before. It's almost as if they knew what dire fate awaited them and are so thankful to you. Shih Tzu, known for their people-pleasing personalities, seem to embody this mentality whole-heartedly when they're rescued. And they want to give something back.

Another perk: Almost all adopted dogs come fully vetted, with proper medical treatment, vaccinations, medicine and are usually already spayed or neutered. Some are even licensed and microchipped.

Don't disregard older dogs, thinking the only good pair-up is you and a puppy. Adult Shih Tzu have more stable behaviors and personalities, helping to better mesh their characteristics with yours in this game of matchmaker. Puppies are always in high demand, so if you open your options to include adult dogs, you'll have a better chance of adopting quickly. Plus, adult dogs are often housetrained, more calm, chew-proof and don't need to be taken outside in the middle of the night. Five times. In the pouring rain, no less.

The American Shih Tzu Club offers rescue support information (www.americanshihtzuclub.org) or log onto Petfinder.com (www.petfinder.com). The site's searchable database allows you to find a Shih Tzu puppy in your area who needs a break in the form of a compassionate and caring owner like you. More websites are listed in the Resources chapter on page 166.

first together with their littermates, then you can see how they interact with each other. You may be able to pinpoint which ones are the bullies and which ones are more submissive. In general, look for a puppy who is more interested in you than in his littermates. Then, take each pup individually to a new location away from the rest of the litter. Put the pup down on the ground, walk away and see how he reacts away from the security of his littermates. The pup may be afraid at first, but should gradually recover and start checking out the new surroundings.

D-I-Y TEMPERAMENT TEST

Puppies come with various temperaments to suit just about everyone. If you are looking for a dog who is easily trainable and a good companion to your family, choose a dog with a medium temperament.

Temperament testing can help you determine your potential puppy's disposition. A pup with a medium temperament will have the following reactions to these tests, best conducted when the pup is about 7 weeks.

Step 1. To test a Shih Tzu pup's social interaction with humans and his confidence or shyness in approaching them, coax him toward you by kneeling down and clapping your hands gently. A puppy with a medium temperament will come readily with his tail up or tail down.

Step 2. To test a pup's eagerness to follow you, walk away from him while he is watching you. The pup should readily follow you with his tail up.

Step 3. To see how a Shih Tzu pup handles restraint, kneel down and roll the pup gently on his back. Using a light but firm touch, hold him in this position with one hand for 30 seconds. The pup should settle down after some initial struggle and offer some or steady eye contact.

Step 4. To evaluate a pup's level of social dominance, stand up, then crouch down beside the pup and stroke him from head to tail. A pup with a medium temperament, neither too dominant nor too submissive, should cuddle up to you and lick your face, or squirm and lick your hands.

Breeder Q&A

JOIN OUR ONLINE Club Shih Tzu®

Here are some questions *you* should ask a breeder and the preferred answers you want.

Q. How often do you have litters available?

A. The answer you want to hear is "occasionally" or "once or twice a year." A breeder who doesn't have litters all that often is probably more concerned with the quality of his puppies, rather than making money.

Q. What kinds of health problems have you had with your Shih Tzu?

A. Beware the breeder who says, "none." Every breed has health issues. For Shih Tzu, some health problems include renal dysplasia, luxated patella and portosystemic vascular anomalies.

Get a complete list of questions to ask a Shih Tzu breeder — and the correct answers — on Club Shih Tzu. Log onto **DogChannel.com/Club-ShihTzu** and click on "Downloads."

A responsible Shih Tzu breeder won't send his pups home until they are 12 weeks of age; that way, the pups have time to bond with each other.

Step 5. An additional test of a pup's dominance is to bend over, cradle him under his belly with your fingers interlaced and palms up, and elevate him just off the ground. Hold for 30 seconds. He should not struggle and should be relaxed, or he should struggle and then settle down and lick you.

A HEALTHY PUPPY

To assess a puppy's health, take a deliberate, thorough look at each part of his body. A healthy puppy has bright eyes, a healthy coat, a good appetite and passes firm stool.

Watch for a telltale link between physical and mental health. A healthy Shih Tzu, as with any breed of puppy, will display a happier, more positive attitude than an unhealthy puppy. A pup's belly should not be over extended or hard, as this may be a sign of worms. Also, if you are around the litter long enough to witness a bowel movement, the stool should be solid and the pup should not show any signs of discomfort. Look into the pup's eyes, too. They should be bright and full of life.

When purchasing a puppy, buyers hear from breeders that these dogs are just like any other puppy — times 10! They are very smart, calculating, stubborn and often have their own agendas. If prospective owners

Did You Know? **Properly bred puppies come from parents who were selected based upon their genetic disease profile.** Their mothers should have been vaccinated, free of all internal and external parasites and properly nourished. For these reasons, a visit to the veterinarian who cared for the mother is recommended. The mother can pass on disease resistance to her puppies, which lasts for 8 to 10 weeks.

aren't willing to spend a fair amount of time with a Shih Tzu, then the breed is not for them. This toy breed wants to be with people more than other dogs and is quite like a 7-year-old boy in that he needs attention and consistent positive reinforcement of good behaviors. Once through adolescence, however, a Shih Tzu is the best friend and companion a person or family could have ever hoped for.

PUPPY PARTICULARS

As you search for a healthy Shih Tzu puppy, here are signs to look for when visiting a breeder. When in doubt, ask the breeder which puppy they think has the best personality/temperament to fit your lifestyle.

1. Look at the area where the pups spend most of their time. It is OK if they play outdoors part of the day, but they should sleep indoors at night so the pups can interact with people and become accustomed to hearing ordinary household noises. This builds a solid foundation for a secure, well-socialized puppy. The puppy area should be clean, well-lit, have fresh drinking water and interesting toys that engage the Shih Tzu puppies.

2. Sure, you're only buying one puppy, but make sure to see all of the puppies in the litter. By 5 weeks of age, healthy pups will begin playing with one another and should be lively and energetic. It's OK if they're asleep when you visit, but stay long enough to see them wake up. Once they're up, they shouldn't be lethargic or weak, as this may be a sign of illness.

3. Pups should be confident and eager to greet you. A pup who is shy or fearful and stays in the corner may be sick or inse-

cure. Although some introverted pups come out of their shells later on, many do not. These dogs will always be fearful as adults and are not good choices for an active, noisy family — with or without children — or for people who have never had a dog. These dogs frighten easily and will require a tremendous amount of training and socialization in order to live a happy life.

Choose a pup who is eager to interact with you but reject the one who is either too shy or bossy. These temperament types are a challenge to deal with and require a lot of training. The perfect Shih Tzu pup personality is somewhere between the two extremes.

4. If it's feeding time during your visit, all Shih Tzu pups should be eager to gobble up their food. Refusing to eat may be a sign of illness.

5. The dog's skin should be clean and shiny without any sores or bumps. Puppies should not be biting or scratching at themselves, which could be a symptom of fleas.

6. After 10 to 12 days, their eyes should be open, clear and without any redness or discharge. Pups should not scratch at their eyes because this may cause an infection or signal irritation.

7. Vomiting or coughing more than once is not normal. The Shih Tzu puppy may be ill and should visit the veterinarian as soon as possible.

8. Visit long enough to see the pups eliminate. All stools should be firm without being watery or bloody. These are signs of illness or that a puppy has worms.

9. Shih Tzu puppies should walk or run without limping.

10. A healthy Shih Tzu pup who eats enough should not be skinny. You should be able to slightly feel his ribs, but you should not be able to see his ribs.

BREEDER PAPERS

Everything today comes with an instruction manual. When you purchase a Shih Tzu, it's no different. A reputable breeder should give you a registration application; a sales contract; a health guarantee; the dog's complete health records; a three-, four- or five-generation pedigree; and some general information about behavior, care, conformation, health and training.

Registration Application. This document from the AKC or UKC assigns your puppy a number and identifies the dog by listing his date of birth, the names of the parents and shows that he is registered as a purebred Shih Tzu. It doesn't prove whether or not your dog is a show- or a pet-quality Shih Tzu and doesn't provide any health guarantee.

Sales Contract. Reputable breeders discuss the terms of the contract before asking you to sign it. This is a written understanding of your expectations about your puppy and shows that the breeder cares about the puppy's welfare throughout his life. The contract can include such terms as requiring you to keep your dog indoors at night, spaying or neutering if the puppy is not going to be a show dog, providing routine veterinary care throughout your dog's life, and assurance that you'll feed your dog a healthy diet. Most responsible breeders will ask that you take your dog to obedience classes and that he earn a Canine Good Citizen title on him before he reaches 2 years of age. Many breeders also require new owners to have totally secure fencing and gates around their yard. Some pups will find a way out of the yard if there's even the slightest opening.

Health Guarantee. This includes a letter from a veterinarian stating your puppy has been examined and is healthy. It also states that the breeder will replace your Shih Tzu if he develops a genetic or life-threatening illness during his lifetime.

Health Records. Here's everything you want to know about not only your puppy's health, but his parents', too.

It should include the dates your puppy was vaccinated, dewormed and examined by a veterinarian for signs of heart murmur, plus the parents' test results for the presence or absence of hip and elbow dysplasia, heart problems and luxated patellas.

Pedigree. Breeders should give you a copy of your Shih Tzu's puppy's three-, four- or five-generation pedigree. Many have photos of your dog's ancestors they will proudly share with you.

Information. The best breeders pride themselves on handing over a notebook full of the latest information on Shih Tzu behavior, care, conformation, health and training. Be sure to read it thoroughly because it will provide invaluable information while you raise your Shih Tzu.

A responsible breeder will be happy to provide you with a folder of your puppy's health records, pedigree and extra useful information.

Signs of a Healthy Puppy
Here are a few things you should look for when selecting a puppy from a litter.

1. NOSE: It should be slightly moist to the touch, but there shouldn't be excessive discharge. The puppy should not be sneezing or sniffling constantly.

2. SKIN AND COAT: Your Shih Tzu pup's coat should be soft and shiny, without flakes or excessive shedding. Watch out for patches of missing hair, redness, bumps or sores. The pup should have a pleasant smell. Check for parasites, such as fleas or ticks.

3. BEHAVIOR: A healthy Shih Tzu puppy may be sleepy, but he should not be lethargic. A healthy pup will be playful at times, not isolated in a corner. You should see occasional bursts of energy and interaction with littermates. When it's mealtime, a healthy pup will take an interest in his food.

There are more signs to look for when picking out the perfect Shih Tzu puppy for you. Download the list at **DogChannel.com/Club-ShihTzu**

ESSENTIALS

Don't think for one second a Shih Tzu would prefer to live in a place described as a box or pen. He wants to live in the Imperial Palace with plenty of toys, soft bedding and other luxuries. Your home is now his home, too. And before you bring a new puppy or rescue dog into his new forever home, you need to make it accessible and comfortable for him.

In fact, in order for him to grow into a stable, well-adjusted dog, he has to feel safe in his surroundings. Remember, he is leaving the warmth and security of his mother and littermates as well as the familiarity of the only place he has ever known, so it is important to make his transition to your home — his new home — as easy and smooth as possible.

PUPPY-PROOFING

Aside from making sure your Shih Tzu will be comfortable in your home, you also have to ensure that your home is safe, which means taking the proper precautions to keep your pup away from things that are dangerous for him.

it's a Fact

Dangers lurk indoors and outdoors. Keep your curious Shih Tzu from investigating your shed and garage. Antifreeze and fertilizers, such as those you would use for roses, will kill a dog. Keep these items on high shelves that are out of your dog's reach.

A well-stocked toy box should contain three main categories of toys:

1. **action** – anything that you can throw or roll and get things moving
2. **distraction** – durable toys that make dogs work for a treat
3. **comfort** – soft, stuffed little "security blankets"

A smart owner will puppy-proof the home inside and out before bringing his or her Shih Tzu home for the first time. Place breakables out of reach. If he is limited to certain places within the house, keep potentially hazardous items in off-limit areas. If your Shih Tzu is going to spend time in a crate, make sure that there is nothing near it he can reach if he sticks his curious little nose or paws through the openings.

The outside of your home must also be safe. Your pup will want to run and explore the yard, and he should be granted that freedom — as long as you are there to supervise. Do not let a fence give you a false sense of security; you would be surprised at how crafty and persistent a dog can be in figuring out how to dig under a fence or squeeze his way through small holes. The solution is to embed the fence deep into the ground.

Be sure to repair or secure any gaps in the fence. Check the fence periodically to ensure it is in good shape and make repairs as needed; a very determined puppy may work on the same spot until he is able to get through.

The following are a few common problems smart Shih Tzu owners watch out for in the home:

■ **Electrical cords and wiring:** No electrical cord or wiring is safe. Many office-supply stores sell products to keep wires gathered under desks, as well as products that prevent chair wheels (and puppy teeth) from damaging electrical cords. If you have exposed cords and wires, these products aren't very expensive and can be used to keep a pup out of trouble.

■ **Trash cans:** Don't waste your time trying to train your Shih Tzu not to get into the trash. Dogs especially love bathroom trash (i.e., cotton balls, cotton swabs, used razors, dental floss, etc.), all of which are extremely dangerous and can cause your Shih Tzu serious harm. Simply put the garbage behind a cabinet door and use a child-safe lock if necessary. Make sure you always shut the bathroom door.

■ **Household cleaners:** Make sure your Shih Tzu puppy doesn't have access to any of these deadly chemicals. Keep them behind closed cabinet doors, using child-safe locks if necessary.

■ **Pest control sprays and poisons:** Chemicals to control ants or other pests should never be used in the house, if possible. Your pup doesn't have to directly ingest these poisons to become ill; if your dog steps in the poison, he can experience toxic

effects from licking his paws. Roach motels and other poisonous pest traps can also be attractive to dogs, so do not drop these behind couches or cabinets; if there's room for a roach motel, there's room for a determined Shih Tzu.

■ **Fabric:** Here's one you might not think about; some puppies have a habit of licking blankets, upholstery, rugs or carpets. Though this habit seems fairly innocuous, over time the fibers from the upholstery or carpet can accumulate in the dog's stomach and cause a blockage. If you see your dog licking these items, remove the item or prevent him from having contact with it.

■ **Prescriptions, painkillers, supplements and vitamins:** Keep all medications in a cabinet. Also, be very careful when taking your prescription medications, supplements or vitamins. How often have you dropped a pill? With a Shih Tzu, you can be sure that he will be at your feet and snarf up the pill before you can even start to say "No!" Take your own pills carefully and without your Shih Tzu present.

■ **Miscellaneous loose items:** If it's not bolted to the floor, your puppy is likely to give the item a taste test. Socks, coins, children's toys, game pieces, cat bell balls — you name it; if it's on the floor, it's worth a try. Make sure the floors in your home are picked up and free of clutter.

FAMILY INTRODUCTIONS

Everyone in the house will be excited about your puppy's homecoming and will want to pet and play with him, but it is best to make the introduction low-key so as not to overwhelm your Shih Tzu. He will already be apprehensive since it is the first time he has been separated from his mother, litter-mates and the breeder, and the ride to your home is likely to be the first time he has been in a car. The last thing you want to do is smother your Shih Tzu, as this will only frighten him further. This is not to say that human contact is not extremely necessary at this stage because this is the time when a connection between the pup and his human family is formed. Gentle petting and soothing words should help console your Shih Tzu, as well as putting him down and letting him explore on his own (under your watchful eye, of course).

Your dog may approach the family members or may busy himself with exploring for a while. Gradually, each person should spend some time with the pup, one at a time, crouching down to get as close to the Shih Tzu's level as possible and letting him sniff their hands before petting him gently. He definitely needs human attention and he needs to be touched; this is how to form an immediate bond. Just remember that your pup is experiencing a lot of things for the first time, all at once. There are new people, noises, smells and things to investigate, so be gentle, be affectionate and be as comforting as possible.

Before you bring your Shih Tzu home, make sure you don't have anything that can put him in harm's way. Go to Club Shih Tzu and click "Downloads" for a list of poisonous plants and foods to avoid as well as a puppy-proofing checklist: **DogChannel.com/Club-ShihTzu**

JOIN OUR ONLINE Club Shih Tzu®

Plan to keep your Shih Tzu's arrival to your home as low-key as possible so he doesn't become nervous and can instead focus on settling in.

NOTABLE & QUOTABLE *The first thing you should always do before your puppy comes home is to lie on the ground and look around. You want to be able to see everything your puppy is going to see. For the puppy, the world is one big chew toy. — Cathleen Stamm, rescue volunteer in San Diego, Calif.*

PUP'S FIRST NIGHT HOME

You have traveled home with your new puppy safely in his crate. He may have already been to the vet for a thorough check-up — he's been weighed, his papers examined, perhaps he's even been vaccinated and dewormed. Your Shih Tzu has met and licked the whole family, including the excited children and the less-than-thrilled cat. He's explored his area, his new bed, the yard and anywhere else he's permitted. He's eaten his first meal at home and relieved himself in the proper place. Your Shih Tzu has heard lots of new sounds, smelled new friends and has seen more of the outside world than ever before.

SMART TIP!

9-1-1! If you don't know whether the plant, food or "stuff" your Shih Tzu just ate is toxic to dogs, you can call the ASPCA's Animal Poison Control Center (888-426-4435). Be prepared to provide your dog's age and weight, her symptoms — if any — and how much of the plant, chemical or substance she ingested, as well as how long ago you think she came into contact with the substance. The ASPCA charges a consultation fee for this service.

A smart Shih Tzu owner purchases all the essential puppy items beforehand so his Shih Tzu has everything he needs from the get-go.

Everyone who rides in your car has to buckle up — even your Shih Tzu! Your dog can travel in the car inside his crate, or you can use a doggie seat belt. These look like harnesses that attach to your car's seat-belt system.

This was just the first day! He's worn out and is ready for bed — or so you think! Remember, this is your puppy's first night to sleep alone. His mother and littermates are no longer at paw's length and he's scared and lonely. Reassure your new family member, but this is not the time to spoil your Shih Tzu and give in to his inevitable whining.

Puppies whine. They whine to let others know where they are and hopefully to get company out of it. Place your Shih Tzu puppy in his new bed or crate in his room and close

the door. Mercifully, he may fall asleep without a peep. If the inevitable occurs, ignore the whining; he is fine. Do not give in and visit your puppy. Don't worry, he will fall asleep eventually.

Many breeders recommend placing a piece of bedding from your Shih Tzu puppy's former home in his new bed so that he will recognize the scent of his littermates. Others advise placing a warm water bottle in his bed. The latter may be a good idea provided the your doesn't attempt to suckle; he'll get good and wet and may not fall asleep quickly.

Your Shih Tzu's first night can be somewhat terrifying for him and his new family. Remember, you set the tone of nighttime at your house. Unless you want to play with your pup every night at 10 p.m., midnight and 2 a.m., don't initiate the habit. Your family will thank you.

SHOPPING FOR A SHIH TZU

It's fun shopping for a new puppy. From training to feeding and sleeping to playing, your new toy dog will need a few items to make life comfy, easy and fun. Be prepared and visit your local pet-supply store before you bring home your new family member.

◆ **Collar and ID tag:** Accustom your dog to wearing a collar the first day you bring him home. Not only will a collar and ID tag help your pup if he becomes lost, collars are also an important training tool. If your Shih Tzu gets into trouble, the collar will act as a handle, helping you divert him to a more appropriate behavior. Make sure the collar fits snugly enough so your toy dog cannot wriggle out of it but is loose enough so it will not be uncomfortably tight around his neck. You should be able to fit a finger between your pup's neck and the collar. Collars come in many styles, but for starting out, a simple

NOTABLE & QUOTABLE

Playing with toys from puppyhood encourages good behavior and social skills throughout your dog's life. A happy, playful dog is a content and well-adjusted one. Also, because all puppies chew to soothe their gums and help loosen puppy teeth, dogs should always have easy access to several different toys.

— *dog trainer and author Harrison Forbes, Savannah, Tenn.*

SMART TIP!

Keep a crate in your vehicle and take your Shih Tzu along when you visit the drive-thru at the bank or your favorite fast-food restaurant. He can watch people interacting, hear interesting sounds and maybe get a dog treat.

buckle collar with an easy-release snap works great.

◆ **Leash:** For training or just for taking a stroll down the street, a leash is your Shih Tzu's means of exploring the outside world. Like collars, leashes come in a variety of styles and materials. A 6-foot nylon leash is a popular choice because it is lightweight and durable. As your pup grows and gets used to walking on the leash, you may want to purchase a flexible leash. These leads allow you to extend the length to give your dog a broader area to explore or to shorten the length to keep your dog closer to you.

◆ **Bowls:** Your Shih Tzu will need two bowls — one for water and one for food. You may want two sets of bowls, one for inside and one for outside, depending on where your dog will be fed and where he will be spending time.

Bowls should be sturdy enough so that they don't tip over easily. (Most have reinforced bottoms that prevent tipping.) Bowls are usually made of metal, ceramic or plastic and should be easy to clean.

◆ **Crate:** A multipurpose crate serves as a bed, housetraining tool and travel carrier. It also is the ideal doggie den — a bedroom of sorts — your Shih Tzu can retire to when he wants to rest or just needs a break. The crate should be large enough for your toy dog to stand in, turn around and lie down. You

Shih Tzu are curious little dogs and will get into everything, so store all potentially harmful items out of the way.

don't want any more room than this — especially if you're planning on using the crate to housetrain your dog because he will eliminate in one corner and lie down in another. Get a crate that is big enough for your dog when he is an adult. Then, use dividers to limit the space for when he's a puppy.

◆ **Bed:** A plush doggie bed will make sleeping and resting more comfortable for your Shih Tzu. Dog beds come in all shapes,

Funny Bone

To err is human, to forgive, canine.

— *Anonymous*

Aside from the basic care items, your Shih Tzu will need plenty of toys to keep him entertained.

sizes and colors, but your dog just needs one that is soft and large enough for him to stretch out on. Because puppies and rescue dogs often don't come housetrained, it's helpful to buy a bed that can be easily washed. If your Shih Tzu will be sleeping in a crate, a nice crate pad and a small blanket that he can burrow in will help him feel more at home. Replace the blanket if it becomes ragged and starts to fall apart because your toy dog's nails could get caught in it.

◆ **Gate:** Similar to those used for toddlers, gates help keep your puppy confined to one room or area when you can't supervise him. Gates also work to keep your dog out of areas you don't want him in. Gates are available in many styles, but for toy dogs, make sure the gate you choose has small bars or openings so your puppy can't squeeze through them.

◆ **Toys:** Keep your dog occupied and entertained by providing him with an array of fun, engaging toys. Teething puppies like to chew — in fact, chewing is a physical need for pups as they are teething — and everything from your shoes to the leather couch to the fancy area rug are fair game.

When you are unable to watch your Shih Tzu puppy, put him in a crate or an exercise pen with a cleanable floor. If she does have an accident on carpeting, clean it thoroughly, so that it doesn't smell like her potty and keep her returning to that spot.

Divert your toy dog's chewing instincts with durable toys like bones made of nylon or hard rubber.

Other fun toys include rope toys, treat-dispensing toys and balls. Make sure the toys and bones don't have small parts that could break off and be swallowed, causing your dog to choke. Stuffed toys can become destuffed and an overly excited Shih Tzu pup may ingest the stuffing or the squeaker. Check your Shih Tzu's toys regularly and replace them if they become frayed or show signs of wear.

◆ **Cleaning supplies:** Until your toy dog pup is housetrained, you will be doing a lot of cleaning. Accidents will occur, which is acceptable in the beginning because the puppy doesn't know any better. All you can do is be prepared to clean up any accidents. Old rags, towels, newspapers and a stain-and-odor remover are good to have on hand.

BEYOND THE BASICS

The items previously discussed are the bare necessities. You will find out what else you need as you go along — grooming supplies, flea and tick protection, etc. These things will vary depending on your situation, but it is important that you have everything you need to make your Shih Tzu comfortable in his new home.

Imagine your beautiful Shih Tzu strolling down the sidewalk; a sturdy, flexible leash is a must!

Some ordinary household items make great toys for your toy dog — as long you make them safe. Tennis balls, plastic water bottles, old towels and more can be transformed into fun with a little creativity. You can find a list of homemade toys at **DogChannel.com/Club-ShihTzu** — click "Downloads."

HOUSETRAINING

Unexciting as it may be, the housetraining part of puppy rearing greatly affects the budding relationship between a smart owner and his puppy — particularly when it becomes an area of ongoing contention. Fortunately, with knowledge, patience and common sense, you'll find housetraining progresses at a relatively smooth rate. That leaves more time for the important things, like cuddling your adorable puppy, showing him off and laughing at his hilarious antics.

Successful housetraining begins with total supervision and management until you know your dog has developed a preference for outside surfaces — grass, gravel, concrete — instead of carpet, tile or hardwood. Crates, tethers, exercise pens and leashes are tools that will help accomplish this. Be consistent, and your puppy will soon know that pottying should occur outside.

IN THE BEGINNING

For the first two to three weeks of a puppy's life, his mother helps him to eliminate. His mother also keeps the whelping box, or "nest area," clean. When pups begin

> **it's a Fact**
> Ongoing housetraining difficulties may indicate that your Shih Tzu puppy has a health problem, warranting a veterinary checkup. A urinary infection, parasites, a virus and other nasty issues greatly affect your puppy's ability to hold it.

The most important element in housetraining your Shih Tzu is patience; this virtue makes the process much smoother.

to walk around and eat on their own, they choose where they eliminate. You can train your puppy to relieve himself wherever you choose, but it must be somewhere suitable. Keep in mind from the start that when your puppy is old enough to go out in public places, any canine deposits must be removed at once; always carry a small plastic bag or poop scoop with you on your outings.

When deciding on the surface and location that you will want your Shih Tzu to use, be sure it is going to be permanent. Training your dog on grass and then changing two months later will be extremely difficult for your Shih Tzu to comprehend.

Next, choose the cue you will use each and every time you want your puppy to potty. "Let's go," "hurry up" and "potty" are examples of cues commonly used by smart dog owners. Get in the habit of giving your Shih Tzu puppy the chosen relief cue before you take him out; that way, when he becomes an adult, you will be able to determine if he wants to go out to potty when you ask him. A confirmation will be signs of interest, such as wagging his tail, turning in circles, barking, watching you intently or going to the door.

LET'S START WITH THE CRATE

Dogs are clean animals by nature, and they dislike soiling where they sleep and eat. This fact makes a crate a useful tool for housetraining. Choose an appropriately sized crate that has adequate room for an adult dog to stand full-height, lie on his side without scrunching and turn around easily. If debating plastic versus wire crates, short-haired breeds sometimes prefer the warmer, draft-blocking quality of plastic while furry dogs often like the cooling airflow of a wire crate.

Some crates come equipped with a movable wall that reduces the interior size to provide enough space for your puppy to stand, turn and lie down, but that do not allow room to soil one end and sleep in the other. The problem is, if your puppy potties in the crate anyway, the divider forces him to lie in his own excrement. This can work against you by desensitizing your puppy against his normal, instinctive revulsion to resting where he has eliminated. If scheduling permits you or a responsible family member to clean the crate soon after it's soiled, then you can continue cratetraining because limiting crate size does encourage your Shih Tzu puppy to hold it. Otherwise, give him enough room to move away from an unclean area until he's better able to control his urge to potty.

Needless to say, not every puppy adheres to this guideline. If your puppy moves along at a faster pace, thank your lucky stars. Should he progress slower, accept it and remind yourself that he'll improve. Be aware that pups frequently hold it longer at night than during the day. Just because your puppy

Always thoroughly clean up your dog's accidents. Left behind scent can draw a dog back to the spot and make him think it's an approved potty area.

sleeps for six or more hours through the night, does not mean he can hold it that long during the day.

One last bit of advice on the crate: Place it in the corner of a normally trafficked room, such as the family room or kitchen. Social and curious by nature, dogs like to feel included in family happenings. Creating a quiet retreat by putting the crate in an unused area may seem like a good idea, but it will result in your puppy feeling insecure and isolated. Watching his people pop in and out of his crate room reassures your puppy he's not forgotten.

Remember that one of the primary ingredients in housetraining your puppy is control. Regardless of your lifestyle, there will always be occasions when you will need to have a place where your dog can stay and be happy and safe. Cratetraining is the answer for now and in the future.

PUPPY'S NEEDS

Your puppy needs to relieve himself after play periods, after each meal, after he has been sleeping and any time he indicates that he is looking for a place to urinate or defecate.

The urinary and intestinal tract muscles of very young puppies are not fully developed. Therefore, like human babies, puppies need to relieve themselves frequently. Take your puppy out often — every hour for an 12-week-old, for example. The older the puppy, the less often he will need to relieve himself. As a mature, healthy adult,

he will require only three to five relief trips per day.

HOUSING HELPS

Because the types of housing and control you provide for your Shih Tzu puppy have a direct relationship on the housetraining success, you must consider the various aspects of both before beginning training. Taking a new puppy home and turning him loose in your house can be compared to turning a child loose in a sports arena and telling the child that the place is all his! The sheer enormity of the place would be too much for him to handle. Instead, offer your puppy clearly

NOTABLE & QUOTABLE

Reward your pup with a high-value treat immediately after she potties to reinforce going in the proper location; then, play for a short time afterward. This teaches that good things happen after pottying outside!

— *Victoria Schade a certified pet dog trainer from Annandale, Va.*

If you acquire your puppy at 12 weeks of age, expect to take her out at least six to eight times a day. By the time she's about 6 months old, potty trips will be down to three or four times a day. A rule of thumb is to take your puppy out in hourly intervals equal to her age in months.

defined areas where he can play, sleep, eat and live. A room of the house where the family gathers is the most obvious choice. Puppies are social animals and need to feel like they are a part of the pack right from the start. Hearing your voice and watching you while you are doing things reinforces his status as a member of your pack.

Usually a family room, the kitchen or a nearby adjoining area is ideal for providing safety and security for puppy and owner.

Within that room, there should be a smaller area that your Shih Tzu puppy can call his own. An alcove, a wire or fiberglass dog crate or a fenced (not boarded!) corner from which he can view the activities of his new family will be fine. The size of the area or crate is the key factor here. The area must be large enough for the puppy to lie down and stretch out his body, yet small enough so he cannot relieve himself at one end and sleep at the other without coming into contact with his droppings before he is fully trained to relieve himself outside.

Dogs will not remain close to their relief areas unless forced to do so. In those cases, going against their instinct will become a habit for life.

Your Shih Tzu's designated area should be lined with clean bedding and should have a toy inside. Water must always be available, in a no-spill container, once your dog is reliably housetrained.

IN CONTROL

By control, we mean helping your puppy to create a lifestyle pattern that will be compatible with that of his pack (that's you!). Just as we guide children to learn our way of life, we must show our pup when it is time to play, eat, sleep, exercise and entertain himself.

Your puppy should always sleep in his crate. He should also learn that, during times of household confusion and excessive human activity, such as at breakfast when family members are preparing for the day, he can play by himself in relative safety and in the comfort of his designated area. Each time you leave your Shih Tzu alone, he should

Did You Know? White vinegar is a good odor remover if you don't have any professional cleaners on hand. Use one-quarter cup mixed with one quart of water.

SMART TIP!

When proximity prevents you from going home at lunch or during periods when overtime crops up, make alternative arrangements for getting your puppy out. Hire a pet sitting or walking service, or enlist the aid of an obliging neighbor.

understand exactly where he is to stay.

Other times of excitement, such as parties, can be fun for your dog, provided that he can view the activities from the security of his designated area. This way, your dog is not underfoot and he is not being fed all sorts of table scraps that will probably cause him stomach distress, yet he still feels a part of the fun.

SCHEDULE A SOLUTION

Your puppy should be taken to his relief area each time he is released from his designated area, after meals, after play sessions and when he first awakens in the morning (at 12 weeks old, this can mean 5 a.m.!). Your Shih Tzu puppy will indicate that he's ready "to go" by circling or sniffing busily; do not misinterpret these signs. As the puppy grows older, he will be able to wait for longer periods of time without having to eliminate.

Keep trips to your puppy's relief area short. Stay no more than five or six minutes, then return to the house. If he goes during that time, praise him lavishly and immediately take him indoors. If he does not, but he has an accident when you go back indoors, pick him up immediately, say "No!" and return to his relief area. Wait a few minutes, then return to the house again. Never spank your puppy or rub his face in urine or excrement when he has

had an accident — or for any other reason, for that matter!

Once indoors, put your Shih Tzu puppy in his crate until you have had time to clean up his accident. Then release him to the family area and watch him more closely than before. Chances are, his accident was a result of your not picking up his potty signals or waiting too long before offering him the opportunity to relieve himself. Never hold a grudge against your puppy for accidents.

Let the puppy learn that going outdoors means it is time to relieve himself,

10 HOUSETRAINING HOW-TOs

1. Decide where you want your dog to eliminate and take her there every time until she gets the idea. Pick a spot that's easy to access; remember, puppies have very little time between "gotta go" and "oops."

2. Teach an elimination cue, such as "go potty" or "get busy." Say this every time you take your Shih Tzu to eliminate. Don't keep chanting the cue, just say it once or twice, then keep quiet so you won't distract your dog.

3. Calmly praise your dog when she eliminates, but stand there a little longer in case there's more.

4. Keep potty outings for potty only. Take your dog to the designated spot, tell her "go potty" and just stand there. If she needs to eliminate, she will do so within five minutes.

5. Don't punish for potty accidents; punishment can hinder progress. If you catch your Shih Tzu in the act indoors, verbally interrupt but don't scold. Gently lead your pup to the approved spot, let her finish, then praise.

6. If it's too late to interrupt an accident, scoop the poop or blot up the urine with a paper towel. Immediately take your Shih Tzu and her deposit (gently!) to the potty area.

Place the poop or trace of urine on the ground and praise the pup. If she sniffs at her waste, praise more. Let your dog know you're pleased when her waste is in the proper area.

7. Keep track of when and where your Shih Tzu eliminates. That will help you anticipate potty times. Regular meals mean regular elimination, so feed your dog scheduled, measured meals instead of free-feeding (leaving food available at all times).

8. Hang a bell on a sturdy cord from the doorknob. Before you open the door to take your dog out for potty, shake the string and ring the bell. Most dogs will soon realize the connection between the bell ringing and the door opening, then they'll try it out for themselves. Listen for that bell!

9. Dogs naturally return to where they've previously eliminated, so thoroughly clean up all accidents. Household cleaners will usually do the job, but special enzyme solutions may work better.

10. If the ground is littered with too much waste, your toy dog may seek a cleaner place to eliminate. Scoop the potty area daily, leaving just one "reminder."

If you decide to papertrain your pup, be consistent with this method so as not to confuse him.

not to play. Once trained, he will be able to play indoors and out and differentiate between the times for play versus the times for relief.

A smart owner will help his or her Shih Tzu puppy develop regular hours for naps, being alone, playing by himself and simply resting, all in his crate. Encourage him to entertain himself while you are busy. Let him learn that having

you nearby is comforting, but it is not your main purpose in life to provide him with undivided attention.

Each time you put your Shih Tzu puppy in his own area, use the same cue, whatever suits you best. Soon he will run to his crate or special area when he hears you say those special words.

A few key elements are really all you need for a successful housetraining method — consistency, frequency, praise, control and supervision. By following these procedures with a normal, healthy puppy, you and your Shih Tzu will soon be past the stage of accidents and ready to move on to a full, rewarding life together. Then, you can start on the more enjoyable aspects of training.

it's a Fact

Dogs are descendants of wolves. So you can think of your Shih Tzu's crate as a modern-day den.

Your dog's crate should be a safe and comfortable place for him as well as a housetraining tool. Don't use it to punish him.

Having housetraining problems with your Shih Tzu? Ask other Shih Tzu owners for advice and tips. Log onto **DogChannel.com/ Club-ShihTzu** and click on "Community."

CHAPTER 6

VET VISITS AND

EVERYDAY CARE

Your selection of a veterinarian should be based on personal recommendation considering the doctor's skills with dogs, specifically Shih Tzu if possible. Following are important things to keep in mind while you search for a veterinarian whom you can trust to care for your precious Shih Tzu.

FIRST STEP: SELECT THE RIGHT VET

All licensed veterinarians are capable of dealing with routine medical issues, such as infections and injuries, and administer vaccinations. If the problem affecting your Shih Tzu is more complex, your vet will refer you to someone with more detailed knowledge of what is wrong. This usually will be a specialist like a veterinary dermatologist, veterinary ophthalmologist or whichever specialty service you require.

Veterinary procedures are very costly and, as the available treatments improve, they are only going to become more expensive. It is quite acceptable to discuss matters of cost with your vet; if there is more than one treatment option, cost may be a factor in deciding which treatment route to take.

Smart owners will look for a veterinarian before they actually need one. New pet owners should start looking for a veterinarian a month or two before they bring home a new Shih Tzu puppy. This will give them time to meet candidate veterinarians, check out the condition of the clinic, meet the staff and see who they feel most comfortable with. If you already have a Shih Tzu puppy, look sooner rather than later, preferably not in the midst of a veterinary health crisis.

Second, define the criteria that are important to you. Points to consider or investigate:

Convenience: Proximity to your home, extended hours or drop-off services are helpful for owners who work regular business hours, who have a busy schedule or who do not want to drive far. If you have mobility issues, finding a vet who makes house calls or a service that provides pet transport might be particularly important.

Size: A one-person practice ensures you will always deal with the same vet during each visit. "That person can really get to know both you and your dog," says Bernadine Cruz, D.V.M., of Laguna Hills Animal Hospital in Laguna Hills, Calif. The downside, though, is that the sole practitioner does not have the immediate input of another vet, and if your vet becomes ill or takes time off, you may be out of luck.

The multiple-doctor practice offers consistency if your Shih Tzu needs to come in unexpectedly on a day when your veterinarian isn't there. Additionally, your vet can quickly consult with his colleagues within the clinic if he's unsure about a diagnosis or a treatment.

If you find a veterinarian within that practice whom you really like, you can make your appointments with that individual, establishing the same kind of bond that you would with a solo practitioner.

Appointment Policies: Some veterinarian practices are strictly by-appointment only, which could minimize your wait time. However, if a sudden problem arises with your Shih Tzu and the veterinarians are booked, they might not be able to squeeze your dog in that day. Some clinics are walk-in only, great for crisis or impromptu visits, but without scheduling, they can involve longer waits to see the next available veterinarian — whoever is open, not someone in particular. Some practices offer the best of both worlds by maintaining an appointment schedule but also keep slots open throughout the day for walk-ins.

Basic vs. State-of-the-Art vs. Full Service: A practice with high-tech equipment offers greater diagnostic capabilities and treatment options, important for tricky or difficult cases. However, the cost of pricey equipment is passed along to the client, so you could pay more for routine procedures —

---

the bulk of most pets' appointments. Some practices offer boarding, grooming, training classes and other services on the premises — conveniences many pet owners appreciate.

Fees and Payment Polices: How much does a routine office call cost? If there is a significant price difference, ask why. If you intend to carry health insurance on your Shih Tzu or want to pay by credit card, make sure the candidate clinic accepts those payment options.

FIRST VET VISIT

It is much easier, less costly and more effective to practice preventive healthcare than to fight bouts of illness and disease. Properly bred puppies of all breeds come from parents who were selected based upon their genetic disease profile. The puppies' mother should have been vaccinated, free of all internal and external parasites and properly nourished. For these reasons, a visit to the veterinarian who cared for the dam (mother) is recommended if at all possible. The dam passes her disease resistance to her puppies, which should last from eight to 10 weeks. Unfortunately, she can also pass on parasites and infection. This is why knowledge about her health is useful in learning more about the health of her puppies.

Now that you have your puppy home safe and sound, it's time to schedule your pup's first veterinary check-up. Perhaps the breeder can recommend someone who specializes in Shih Tzu, or maybe you know other Shih Tzu owners who can suggest a good vet. Either way, make an appointment within a couple of days of bringing home your puppy. If possible, stop by for this first vet appointment before going home.

Did You Know?

Obesity is linked to an earlier onset of age-related health problems. Keep weight in check by providing sufficient exercise and play, and by feeding proper serving sizes. Calorie requirements decline as your puppy reaches adulthood and can drop 25 to 30 percent within a couple of months after your dog has been spayed or neutered; you'll probably need to reduce serving portions and switch to a less calorie-dense diet.

The pup's first vet visit will consist of an overall examination to make sure that he does not have any problems that are not apparent to you. The veterinarian also will set up a schedule for your pup's vaccinations; the breeder will inform you of which ones your dog has already received and the vet can continue from there.

Your Shih Tzu will also have his teeth examined and have his skeletal conformation and general health checked prior to certification by the veterinarian. Puppies in certain breeds have problems with their kneecaps, cataracts and other eye problems, heart murmurs and undescended testicles. They may also have personality problems; your veterinarian might even have training in temperament evaluation.

VACCINATION SCHEDULING

Most vaccinations are given by injection and should only be given by a veterinarian. Both you and the vet should keep a record of the date of the injection, the identification of the vaccine and the amount given. Some vets give a first vaccination at 8 weeks of age, but most dog breeders prefer the course not to commence until about 10 weeks because of interaction with the antibodies produced by the mother. The vaccination scheduling is usually based on a 15-day cycle. You must take your vet's advice as to when to vaccinate, as this may differ according to the vaccine used.

The usual vaccines contain immunizing doses of several different viruses such as distemper, parvovirus, parainfluenza and hepatitis. There are other vaccines available when the puppy is at risk; you should rely on your vet's advice. This is especially true for the booster immunizations. Most vaccination programs require a booster when the puppy is a year old and once a year thereafter. In some cases, circumstances may require more frequent immunizations.

Kennel cough, more formally known as *tracheobronchitis*, is immunized with a vaccine that is sprayed into a dog's nostrils. Kennel cough is usually included in routine vaccinations, but it's usually not as effective as vaccines for other diseases.

Your veterinarian probably will recommend that your Shih Tzu puppy be fully vaccinated before you take him on outings. There are airborne diseases, parasite eggs in the grass and unexpected visits from other

Set up a vet visit before you bring your new dog home, so you can meet and interview the veterinarian staff.

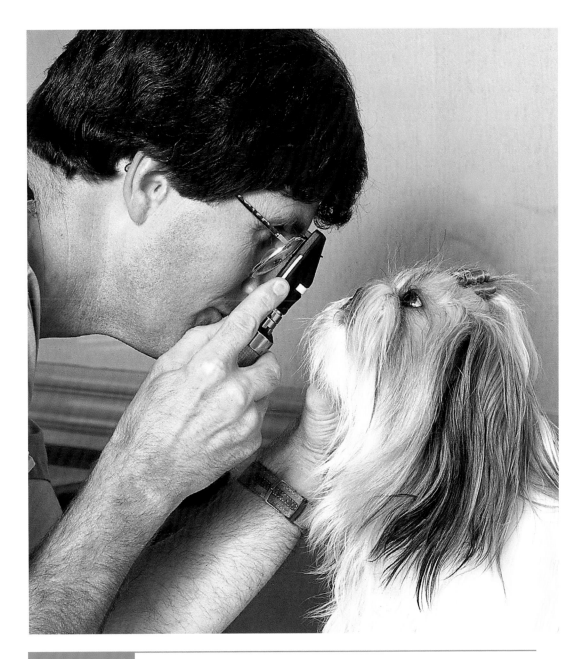

When you first get your dog, consult your veterinarian or a veterinary ophthalmologist about possible issues concerning her eyes. As a prevention, most Shih Tzu could benefit from lifelong tear supplementation. A wet eye is a happy eye!

— Dr. Dan W. Lorimer, of Michigan Veterinary Specialists in Southfield, Mich.

During your puppy's first few weeks at home, take him to the vet just to meet the staff and get to know the office.

dogs that might be dangerous to your puppy's health. Other dogs are the most harmful reservoir of pathogenic organisms, as everything they have can be transmitted to your puppy.

6 Months to 1 Year of Age: Unless you intend to breed or show your dog in the ring, neutering or spaying your puppy at 6 months of age is recommended. Discuss this with your veterinarian. Neutering or spaying has proven to be beneficial to male and female puppies, respectively. Besides eliminating the possibility of pregnancy, it inhibits (but does not prevent) breast cancer in females and prostate cancer in male dogs.

Your veterinarian should provide your Shih Tzu puppy with a thorough dental evaluation at 6 months of age to ascertain whether all your Shih Tzu's permanent teeth have come in properly. A home dental care regimen should be implemented at this time, including weekly teeth cleanings and providing good dental devices (such as nylon bones). Regular dental care promotes healthy teeth, fresh breath, a healthy heart and a longer life.

Small, brachycephalic dogs are more prone to dental disorders. First, they have large-sized teeth, which cause crowding and favor the accumulation of plaque that cause periodontal disease. Second, their protruding lower jaws (caused, actually, by a small upper jaw) result in malpositioned teeth and further crowding that predisposes them to periodontitis.

— Dr. Daniel T. Carmichael, a diplomate of the American Veterinary Dental College at The Center for Specialized Veterinary Care in Westbury, N.Y.

When selecting a veterinarian, make sure he or she is familiar with Shih Tzu.

Dogs Older Than 1 Year: Continue to visit the veterinarian at least once a year. There is no such disease as "old age," but bodily functions do change as your dog gets older. The eyes and ears are no longer as efficient, and liver, kidney and intestinal functions begin to decline. Proper dietary changes, recommended by your veterinarian, can make life more pleasant for your aging Shih Tzu and you.

EVERYDAY HAPPENINGS

Keeping your Shih Tzu healthy is a matter of keen observation and quick action when necessary. Knowing what's normal for your dog will help you recognize signs of trouble before they blossom into a full-blown emergency situation.

Even if the problem is minor, such as a cut or scrape, you'll want to care for it immediately to prevent infection, as well as to ensure that your Shih Tzu doesn't make it worse by chewing or scratching at it.

Here's what to do for common, minor injuries or illnesses and how to recognize and deal with emergencies:

Cuts and Scrapes: For a cut or a scrape that's half an inch or smaller, clean the

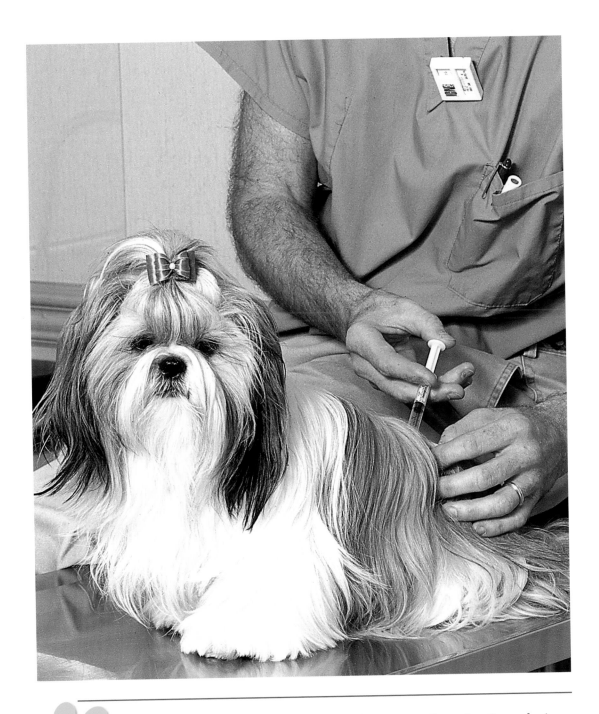

Just like with infants, puppies need a series of vaccinations during their first year of life to ensure that they stay healthy. Download a vaccination chart from **DogChannel.com/Club-ShihTzu** that you can fill out for your Shih Tzu.

wound with saline solution or warm water and use tweezers to remove any splinters or other debris. Apply antibiotic ointment. No bandage is necessary unless the wound is on a paw, which can pick up dirt when your dog walks on it. Deep cuts with lots of bleeding or those caused by glass or some other object should be treated by your veterinarian.

Cold Symptoms: Dogs don't actually get colds, but they can get illnesses that have similar symptoms, such as coughing, a runny nose or sneezing. Dogs cough for any number of reasons, from respiratory infections to inhaled irritants to congestive heart failure. Take your Shih Tzu to the veterinarian for prolonged coughing or coughing accompanied by labored breathing, runny eyes or nose or bloody phlegm.

A runny nose that continues for more than several hours requires veterinary attention, as well. If your Shih Tzu sneezes, he may have some mild nasal irritation that will go away on its own, but frequent sneezing, especially if it's accompanied by a runny nose, may indicate anything from allergies to an infection to something stuck in the nose.

Vomiting and Diarrhea: Sometimes dogs suffer minor gastric upsets when they eat a new type of food, eat too much, eat the contents of the trash can or become excited or anxious. Give your Shih Tzu's stomach a rest by withholding food for 12 hours, and then feeding him a bland diet such as baby food, or rice and chicken, gradually returning your Shih Tzu to his normal food. Projectile vomiting, or vomiting or diarrhea that continues for more than 48 hours, is another matter. If this happens, immediately take your Shih Tzu to the veterinarian.

MORE HEALTH HINTS

A Shih Tzu's anal glands can cause problems if not periodically evacuated. In the wild, dogs regularly clear their anal glands to mark their territory, but in domestic dogs this function is no longer necessary; thus, their contents can build up and clog, causing discomfort. Signs that the anal glands — located on both sides of the anus — need emptying are if a Shih Tzu drags his rear end along the ground or keeps turning around to attend to the uncomfortable patch.

While care must be taken not to cause injury, anal glands can be evacuated by gently pressing on either side of the anal opening and by using a piece of cotton or a tissue to collect the foul-smelling matter. If anal glands are allowed to become impacted, abscesses can form, causing pain and the need for veterinary attention.

Shih Tzu can get into all sorts of mischief, so it's not uncommon for them to inadvertently swallow something poisonous in the course of their investigations. Obviously, an urgent visit to your vet is required under such circumstances, but if possible, when you telephone him or her, you should advise which poisonous substance has been ingested, as different treatments are needed.

Should it be necessary to cause your dog to vomit (which is not always the case with poisoning), a small lump of baking soda, given orally, will have an immediate effect. Alternatively, a teaspoon of salt or mustard, dissolved in water, will have a similar effect but may be more difficult to administer and not as quick to take effect.

Shih Tzu puppies often have painful fits while they are teething. These are not usually serious and are brief, caused only by the pain of teething. Of course, you must be certain that the cause is not more serious. Giving a puppy something hard to chew on will usually be enough to solve this temporary teething problem.

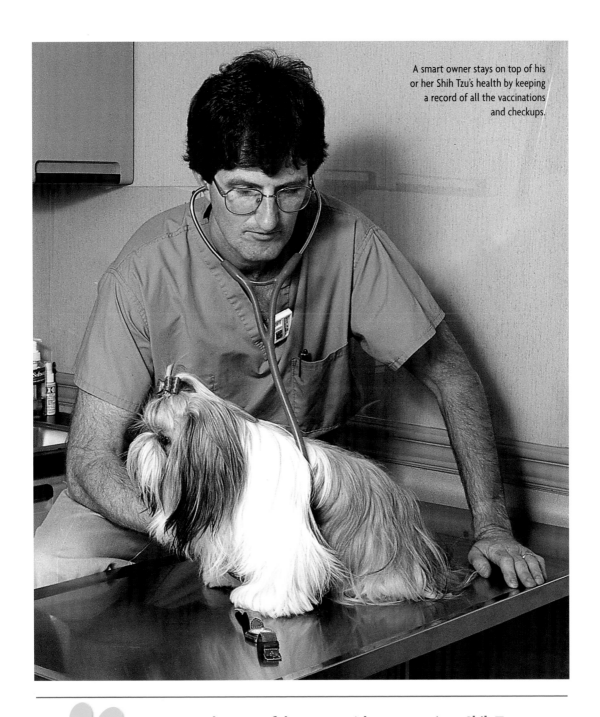

A smart owner stays on top of his or her Shih Tzu's health by keeping a record of all the vaccinations and checkups.

No matter how careful you are with your precious Shih Tzu, sometimes unexpected injuries happen. Be prepared for any emergency by assembling a canine first-aid kit. Find out what essentials you need on **DogChannel.com/Club-ShihTzu** — just click on "Downloads."

OF HEALTH

The best way to ensure good health for your Shih Tzu is by maintaining a consistent wellness program. Take your dog in for regular veterinary exams; stay current with vaccinations and flea or heartworm prevention (per your veterinarian's recommendation); keep your Shih Tzu's skin and coat groomed; brush your dog's teeth regularly; and seek prompt veterinary attention if he exhibits physical or behavioral changes.

The latter is a key component to your dog's health. Staying on top of problems via early diagnosis and treatment often yields the best prognosis, by correcting a problem before it becomes severe, permanent or life-ending, by helping slow disease progression and possibly extending your dog's life.

Although the Shih Tzu is a healthy breed with a lifespan of about 12 to 14 years, the breed is not immune to genetic problems — no dog is. In fact, all domestic and wild mammals, including humans, carry some defective genes that may or may not manifest into full-blown disease. Some disorders seen in Shih Tzu include renal dysplasia, portosystemic vascular anomalies and luxated patella. Here is an introduction to what these diseases are and how you can best manage them.

Did You Know?

Dogs can get many diseases from ticks, including Lyme disease, Rocky Mountain spotted fever, tick bite paralysis and many others.

RENAL DYSPLASIA

A deadly disease, renal dysplasia is a developmental abnormality of the kidneys. The kidneys fail to fully develop; fetal kidney tissue fails to be entirely replaced by adult kidney tissue. The end result of renal dysplasia is the same as kidney disease: renal failure.

An inherited disease, about 30 percent of all Shih Tzu carry the gene for renal dysplasia, according to research provided by Michigan State University. However, incidence of the disease itself is between $2\frac{1}{2}$ and 4 percent of the Shih Tzu population.

The onset of clinical signs is variable, and happens between 4 weeks of age to more than 5 years. However, most cases progress to renal failure before the dog is 2 years of age. Early signs of renal failure include lethargy, selective appetite, poor hair coat, stunted growth, and increased water consumption and urination. In severe cases of renal dysplasia, or as the failure progresses, clinical signs become more severe and include prolonged loss of appetite, depression, vomiting, diarrhea, dehydration, bad breath, mouth sores, pale gums, severe weight loss and sometimes bone fractures due to pathologic (nontraumatic) causes.

SMART TIP!

Many skin irritations can be prevented or reduced by employing a simple preventative regimen:
- Keep your Shih Tzu clean and dry.
- Bathe your Shih Tzu regularly (particularly during allergy season) with a hypoallergenic shampoo.
- Rinse her coat thoroughly.
- Practice good flea control.
- Supplement her diet with fatty acids.

Kidney disease diagnosis is based upon the dog's history, clinical signs noticed by the owner, physical exam, bloodwork and urinalysis. Abdominal palpation may reveal small, irregularly shaped kidneys. The veterinarian may also perform abdominal radiography or abdominal ultrasound to document abnormal renal shape, size and architecture. The actual diagnosis of renal dysplasia as the underlying cause is usually presumptive, based on the dog's age. A definitive diagnosis of renal dysplasia requires kidney biopsy, but because all kidney disease is treated in the same manner, that knowledge would not alter the treatment regimen or outcome.

PORTOSYSTEMIC VASCULAR ANOMALIES

PSVA, or liver shunt, is a very serious liver developmental birth defect. Some clinical signs include disorientation, wobbly or weak movements, your dog pressing his head against the wall and walking in circles. If left untreated, PSVA often develops into progressive liver disease, liver failure or death. This disease is more common in small dogs.

Normally, blood flows through the liver, allowing the liver to do its job of maintaining body metabolism, synthesizing proteins and sugars, manufacturing enzymes and removing blood-borne waste products and toxins from the system. For dogs with a PSVA, though, some of the blood bypasses or shunts away from the liver, so the liver does not detoxify that portion of blood as it normally would. In some cases, hundreds to millions of abnormal microscopic shunting vessels are formed, a type of PSVA known as microvascular dysplasia. Clinical signs usually show up before 1 year of age, as early as a few months of age.

Prevention is the best medicine; be sure to take your Shih Tzu to the vet for regular checkups, not just when he is showing signs.

Definitively diagnosing PSVA can be an involved process, requiring a variety of laboratory tests and an ultrasound or colonic scintigraphy (a process were the veterinarian places radioactive compound into the rectum) to identify the shunting vessels or to confirm blood function within the liver.

Depending upon the particular nature of the PSVA abnormalities found in the dog, the veterinarian will either recommend surgery — a very technical and demanding surgical procedure — or treatment and management with medication.

BAD KNEES

Patellar luxation (slipped kneecap), an orthopedic problem seen in many small breeds, is one of the most common causes of lameness. It's usually caused by abnormalities in the patella (a flat, movable bone at the front of the knee) and is hereditary. Generally, the problem starts when the dog is still young, 6 months or younger, although occasionally a dog can be older when the problem first occurs. Trauma can also force the patella out of place — something that can happen at any age.

When the patella luxates, the hind lower leg seems to momentarily lock and the dog "skips" for a stride or two; then the leg drops back into place again and everything seems fine. Often, the skipping occurs while the dog is trotting or right after he stands, turns or jumps.

Depending on how advanced the problem becomes, a dog can experience discomfort, lameness and permanent joint damage, so it's best not to ignore this condition. A veterinary exam is important to confirm the diagnosis (which is based on a physical exam and radiographs) and to evaluate the severity as soon as possible.

In mild cases where the patella only very occasionally dislocates and pops right back into place, there is no residual lameness, very little discomfort and little or no cumulative or permanent damage to the joint, treatment is unnecessary. You should monitor your pet, however, and have him re-evaluated if the luxations become more frequent or the patella stays out of the groove for longer periods of time.

In some cases, the patella luxates more frequently, doesn't slip back into place quickly or the veterinarian determines that the patella pops out too easily. These dogs need surgery to correct the condition and to prevent permanent lameness and joint damage. In these cases, without treatment, a dog will not get better on his own, and the condition could worsen, becoming more painful and causing greater damage to the joint. The more damage a joint undergoes, the more difficult it is to repair the abnormalities and to achieve complete surgical correction.

To prevent over-exercising after surgery, keep your dog on leash when outside to relieve himself and crated at other times. As your dog recovers, leash walks and gradually increasing exercise are permitted, per veterinary evaluation. Usually, dogs complete their recovery in a couple of months. When treated promptly, prognosis for a full recovery is usually good.

EYE AND TEETH ISSUES

Brachycephalic, or short-headed, dogs are susceptible to eye and dental disorders due to their conformation. The Shih Tzu's large, protruding eyes have a greater risk of trauma and abnormal eye lubrication, and their teeth are often crowded or badly aligned.

Eyes: Two common eye disorders are *keratoconjunctivitis sicca* (aka KCS or dye eye), which is due to a reduced tear production, and exposure *keratitis*, an excessive exposure of the cornea due to large eyelid margins. Both involve reduced eye lubrication, leading to eye surface damage, scar-

ring, pain and sometimes vision or eye loss, says Dan W. Lorimer, a diplomate of American College of Veterinary Ophthalmologists, of Michigan Veterinary Specialists in Southfield, Mich.

Other eye problems include *trichiasus* and *distichiasus* where the eyelashes rub against and damage the eye surface, and corneal ulcerations and corneal perforations, due to trauma or secondary to other disorders. Less common eye conditions include cataracts and retinal detachment related to a genetic, but sometimes traumatic, causes.

Symptoms of eye abnormalities vary but can include squinting, ocular discharge, pain, or cloudy or dilated pupils. Depending on the disorder, treatment consists of medication, lubricants, artificial tears or surgery. Prompt treatment is critical for preserving vision; delays could result in increased or irreversible damage, blindness or even eye loss.

Teeth: "Small, brachycephalic dogs are more prone to dental disorders," says Daniel T. Carmichael, a diplomate of the American Veterinary Dental College at The Center for Specialized Veterinary Care in Westbury, N.Y. "First, they have proportionally large-sized teeth, which cause crowding and favor the accumulation of plaque bacteria that cause periodontal disease. Second, their protruding lower jaws (caused, actually, by a small upper jaw) result in malpositioned teeth and further crowding that predisposes them to periodontitis."

Untreated periodontal disease, a progressive infection affecting the attachment of the teeth to the gums, can lead to painful mouth infections, infection in vital body organs and tooth loss, Carmichael states. Bad breath, bleeding gums and loose teeth are common clinical signs. Professional dental cleaning can remove plaque, but advanced cases often require periodontal

Did You Know? Across the globe, more than 800 species of ticks exist, and they aren't particular to where they dine. Mammals, birds and reptiles are all fair game.

surgery or even dental extraction. A vaccine to prevent periodontal disease is under development.

Malpositioned teeth can protrude into the gums, make abnormal tooth contact or prevent mouth closure. This is an often painful condition and can lead to tooth loss. Treatment consists of special canine braces or dental extractions.

Shih Tzu also seem predisposed to dentigerous cysts, benign but expansive jaw lesions that can damage the jaw bone and teeth adjacent to it. The condition often presents as progressive swelling of the jawbone. Surgical removal of the cyst is the only treatment, Carmichael says.

Although Shih Tzu are extremely susceptible to dental disorders, Carmichael notes that daily tooth brushing, dental diet, chew toys and yearly professional dental cleanings will help these dogs keep their teeth for life.

AIRBORNE ALLERGIES

Just as humans suffer from hay fever during the pollinating season, many dogs suffer from the same allergies. When the pollen count is high, your Shih Tzu might suffer, but don't expect him to sneeze or have a runny nose like a human. Dogs react to airborne allergies in the same way they react to parasite bites; they scratch and bite themselves. Dogs, like humans, can be tested for allergens, discuss testing your dog for allergies with your vet.

AUTO-IMMUNE ILLNESS

An auto-immune illness is one in which the immune system overacts and does not recognize parts of the affected dog. Instead, the immune system reacts and turns against the body's cells as if they were foreign cells and must be destroyed. One example is rheumatoid arthritis, which occurs when the body does not recognize the joints, leading to a very painful and damaging reaction. This has nothing to do with age, so it can occur in puppies. The wear-and-tear arthritis in older people or dogs is called *osteoarthritis*.

Lupus is another auto-immune disease that affects dogs as well as people. It can present in a variety of forms, affecting the kidneys, bones and skin. It can be fatal, so it is treated with steroids, which can trigger very harsh side effects.

Steroids slows the allergic reaction to the body's tissues, which helps the lupus, but it also slows down a canine's body's reaction to actual foreign substances such as bacteria, making your dog vulnerable to other illnesses. Steroids also thin the skin and bones.

FOOD ALLERGIES

Feeding your Shih Tzu properly is very important. An improper diet could affect your dog's health, behavior and nervous system, possibly making a normal dog aggressive. The result of a good or bad diet is most visible in a dog's skin and coat, but internal organs are affected, too.

Some dogs are allergic to many foods that are popular and even recommended by breeders and veterinarians. Changing the brand of food may not solve the problem if the ingredient your dog is allergic to is contained in the new brand.

Recognizing a food allergy can be difficult. People often have rashes or swelling of the lips or eyes when they eat foods they are allergic to. Dogs react the same way they do to an airborne or insect bite allergy; they itch, scratch and bite. While pollen allergies and parasite bites are usually seasonal, food allergies are continual.

Food allergy diagnosis is based on a 2- to 4-week dietary trial with a home-cooked diet fed excluding all other foods. The diet should consist of boiled rice or potato and a protein your Shih Tzu has never eaten, such as fresh or frozen fish, lamb or even something as exotic as pheasant. Water has to be the only drink, and it is important that no other foods are fed during this trial. If your dog's condition improves, try the original diet again to see if the itching resumes. If it does, then your dog is allergic to his original diet. You must find a diet that does not distress your dog's skin. Start with a commercial hypoallergenic diet or the homemade diet you created for the allergy trial.

Food intolerance is your dog's inability to completely digest certain foods. This occurs because your dog does not have the enzymes necessary to digest some foods. All puppies have the enzymes necessary to

SMART TIP!

Brush your dog's teeth every day.
Plaque colonizes on the tooth surface in as little as six to eight hours, and if not removed by brushing, forms calculus (tartar) within three to five days. Plaque and tartar cause gum disease, periodontal disease, loosening of the teeth and tooth loss. In bad cases of dental disease, bacteria from the mouth can get into the bloodstream, leading to kidney or heart problems — either of which are life-shortening.

digest canine milk, but some dogs do not have the enzymes to digest cow milk, resulting in loose bowels, stomach pains and flatulence. Dogs often do not have the enzymes to digest soy or other beans. These foods should be excluded from your Shih Tzu's diet.

PARASITE BITES

Insect bites itch, erupt and may even become infected. Dogs have the same reaction to fleas, ticks and mites. When an insect lands on you, you can whisk it away with your hand. Unfortunately, when a dog is bitten by a flea, tick or mite he can only scratch or bite. By the time your Shih Tzu has been bitten, the parasite has done its damage. It may also have laid eggs, which will cause further problems. The itching from parasite bites is probably due to the saliva injected into the site when the parasite sucks the dog's blood.

EXTERNAL PARASITES

Fleas: Of all the problems to which dogs are prone, none is better known and more frustrating than the flea. Flea infestation is relatively simple to cure, but it can be difficult to prevent.

To control flea infestation, you have to understand the flea's life cycle. Fleas are often thought of as a summertime problem, but centrally heated homes have made fleas a year-round problem. The most effective method of treating fleas is a two-stage approach: Kill the adult fleas, then control the development of pre-adult fleas (*pupae*). Unfortunately, no single active ingredient is effective against all stages of the flea life cycle.

Controlling fleas is a two-pronged attack. First, the environment needs to be treated; this includes carpets and furniture, especially your Shih Tzu's bedding and areas underneath furniture. The environment should be treated with a household spray containing an insect growth regulator and an insecticide to kill the adult fleas. Most insecticides are effective against eggs and larvae; they mimic the fleas' own hormones and stop the eggs and larvae from developing into adult fleas. There are currently no treatments available to attack the pupae stage of the life cycle, so the adult insecticide is used to kill the newly hatched fleas before they find a host. Most insect growth regulators are active for many months, while adult insecticides are only active for a few days.

When treating with a household spray, vacuum before applying the product. This stimulates as many pupae as possible to hatch into adult fleas. The vacuum cleaner should also be treated with an insecticide to prevent the eggs and larvae that have been collected in the vacuum bag from hatching.

The second treatment stage is to apply an adult insecticide to your Shih Tzu. Traditionally, this would be in the form of a flea collar or a spray, but more recent innovations include digestible insecticides that poison the fleas when they ingest the dog's blood.

it's a Fact

In young puppies, roundworms cause bloated bellies, diarrhea and vomiting, and are transmitted from the mother (through blood or milk). Affected pups will not appear as animated as normal puppies. The worms appear spaghetti-like, measuring as long as 6 inches!

There are also drops that, when placed on the back of the dog's neck, spread throughout the hair and skin to kill adult fleas.

Ticks: Though not as common as fleas, ticks are found in tropical and temperate climates. They don't bite like fleas; they harpoon. They dig their sharp *proboscis* (nose) into your Shih Tzu's skin and drink the blood, which is their only food and drink. Ticks are controlled the same way fleas are controlled.

The American dog tick, *Dermacentor variabilis*, may be the most common dog tick in many areas, especially those areas where the climate is hot and humid. Most dog ticks have life expectancies of a week to six months, depending on climactic conditions. They can neither jump nor fly, but they can crawl slowly and can travel up to 16 feet to reach a sleeping or unsuspecting dog.

Mites: Just as fleas and ticks can be problematic for your dog, mites can also lead to an itch fit. Microscopic in size, mites are related to ticks and generally take up permanent residence on their host animal — in this case, your Shih Tzu! The term "mange" refers to any infestation caused by one of the mighty mites, of which there

Don't let fleas get your Shih Tzu down. Prevent them before they take hold of your dog (and home!).

are six varieties that smart dog owners should know about.

* The *Cheyletiellosis* mite is the hook-mouthed culprit associated with "walking dandruff," a condition that affects dogs as well as cats and rabbits. If untreated, this mange can affect a whole kennel of dogs and can be spread to humans, as well.

* The *Sarcoptes* mite causes intense itching on the dog in the form of a condition known as scabies or sarcoptic mange. Scabies is highly contagious and can be passed to humans. Sometimes an allergic reaction to the mite worsens the severe itching associated with sarcoptic mange.

* Ear mites, *Otodectes cynotis*, lead to otodectic mange, which commonly affects the outer ear canal of the dog, though other areas can be affected as well. Your vet can prescribe a treatment to flush out the ears and kill any eggs in the ears. A month of treatment is necessary to cure mange.

* Two other mites, that are less common in dogs, include *Dermanyssus galli-nae* (the "poultry" or "red mite") and *Eutrombicula alfreddugesi* (the North American mite associated with *trombicu-lidiasis* or chigger infestation). The types of mange caused by both of these mites must be treated by vets.

INTERNAL PARASITES

Most animals — fish, birds, and mammals, including dogs and humans — have worms and other parasites living inside their bodies. According to Dr. Herbert R. Axelrod, a fish pathologist, there are two kinds of parasites: smart and dumb. The "smart" parasites live in peaceful cooperation with their hosts (symbiosis), while the "dumb" parasites kill their hosts. Most worm infections are relatively easy to control. If they are not controlled, they weaken the host dog to the point that other medical problems occur, but they do not kill the host as "dumb" parasites would.

Roundworms: Roundworms that infect dogs live in the dog's intestines and shed eggs continually. It has been estimated that a dog produces about six or more ounces of feces every day, and each ounce averages hundreds of thousands of roundworm eggs. There are no known areas in which dogs roam that do not contain roundworm eggs. Because roundworms infect people too, it is wise to have your dog regularly tested.

Roundworm infection can kill puppies and cause severe problems in adult dogs, as the hatched larvae travel to the lungs and trachea through the bloodstream. Cleanliness is the best prevention against roundworms. Always pick up after your dog and dispose of feces in appropriate receptacles.

Hookworms: Hookworms are dangerous to humans as well as to dogs and cats, and can be the cause of severe iron-deficiency anemia. The worm uses its teeth to attach itself to the dog's intestines and changes the site of its attachment about six times per day. Each time the worm repositions itself, the dog loses blood and can become anemic.

Symptoms of hookworm infection include dark stools, weight loss, general weakness, pale coloration and anemia as well as possible skin problems. Fortunately, hookworms are easily purged with a number of medications that have proven effective; discuss these with your veterinarian. Most heartworm preventives also include a hookworm insecticide.

Humans, can be infected by hookworms through exposure to contaminated feces. Because the worms cannot complete their life cycle in a human, the worms simply infest the skin and cause irritation. As a preventive, use disposable gloves or a poop-scoop to pick up your dog's droppings. In addition, be sure to prevent your dog (or neighborhood cats) from defecating in children's play areas.

Tapeworms: There are many species of tapeworm, all of which are carried by fleas. Fleas are so small that your Shih Tzu could pass them onto your hands, your plate or your food, making it possible for you to ingest a flea that is carrying tapeworm eggs. While tapeworm infection is not life-threatening in dogs (a smart parasite), it can be the cause of a very serious liver disease in humans.

Whipworms: In North America, whipworms are counted among the most common parasitic worms in dogs. Affected dogs may only experience upset stomachs, colic and diarrhea. These worms, however, can live for months or years in the dog, beginning their larval stage in the small intestine, spending their adult stage in the large intestine and finally passing infective eggs through the dog's feces. The only way to detect whipworms is through a fecal examination, though this is not always foolproof. Treatment for whipworms is tricky, due to the worms' unusual life cycle, and often dogs are reinfected due to infective eggs on the ground. Cleaning up droppings in your backyard and in public places is absolutely essential for sanitation purposes and the health of your dog and others.

Threadworms: Though less common than roundworms, hookworms and previously mentioned parasites, threadworms concern dog owners in the southwestern United States and Gulf Coast area where it is hot and humid.

They live in the small intestine of the dog, measures a mere two millimeters and is round in shape. Like the whipworm, the threadworm's life cycle is very complex, and the eggs and larvae are passed through the feces.

A deadly disease in humans, threadworms readily infect people, mostly through the direct handling of dog feces. Threadworms are most often seen in young puppies. The most common symptoms include bloody diarrhea and pneumonia.

Talk to your veterinarian about worm prevention.

Sick puppies must be isolated and treated immediately; vets recommend a follow-up treatment one month later.

Heartworms: Heartworms are thin, extended worms up to 12 inches long, that live in a dog's heart and the major blood vessels surrounding it. Dogs may have up to 200 heartworms. Symptoms can include loss of energy, loss of appetite, coughing, the development of a pot belly and anemia.

Heartworms are transmitted by mosquitoes, which drink the blood of infected dogs and take in larvae with the blood. The larvae, called microfilariae, develop within the body of the mosquito and are passed on to the next dog bitten after the larvae mature. It takes two to three weeks for the larvae to develop to the infective stage within the body of the mosquito. Dogs are usually treated at about 6 weeks of age and maintained on a prophylactic dose given monthly.

Blood testing for heartworms is not indicative of how seriously your dog is infected. Although this is a dangerous disease, it is not easy for a dog to become infected. Discuss the various preventives with your vet, because there are many different types now available. Together you can decide on a safe course of prevention for your dog.

CHAPTER 8

TIME TO FEED

YOUR TOY

You have probably heard it a thousand times: You are what you eat. Believe it or not, it is very true, especially for dogs. Dogs are what you feed them because they have little choice in the matter. Even smart owners, who truly want to feed their dogs properly, often cannot do so because they don't know which foods are the best and most nutritious.

BASIC TYPES

Dog foods are produced in various types: dry, wet (canned), semimoist and frozen.

Dry food is useful for the cost-conscious owner because it tends to be less expensive than others. This food also contains the least fat and the most preservatives. Dry food is bulky and takes longer to eat than other foods, so it's more filling.

Wet food — available in cans or foil pouches — is usually 60 to 70 percent water and is more expensive than dry food. A palatable source of concentrated nutrition, wet food also makes an excellent supplement for underweight dogs or those recovering from an illness. Some smart owners add a little wet food to dry to increase its appeal. Dogs gobble up this savory mixture.

it's a Fact

Bones can cause gastrointestinal obstruction and perforation and may be contaminated with salmonella or E. coli. Leave them in the trash and give your dog a nylon toy bone instead.

Semimoist food is flavorful but usually contains lots of sugar, which can lead to dental problems and obesity. It's not a good choice for your dog's main diet.

Frozen food, which is available in cooked and raw forms, is usually more expensive than wet food. The advantages of frozen food are similar to those of wet food.

Some manufacturers have developed special foods for small dogs. Some of these contain slightly more protein, fat and calories than standard foods. Manufacturers contend that small dogs need these additional nutrients to fuel their active lifestyle and revved-up metabolism. In reality, your Shih Tzu may or may not need them; the nutritional needs of dogs vary considerably, even within the same breed. It's OK to feed your Shih Tzu small-breed food, but standard food will provide balanced nutrition, too, as long as you feed appropriate amounts tailored to your buddy's needs.

Some dry foods for small dogs have compositions that are identical to those for larger dogs, but the kibble is smaller to make it easier to chew. Small dogs don't really need smaller kibble, though your Shih Tzu may prefer it. Many small dogs eat standard-size kibble with no trouble at all.

The amount of food your toy dog needs depends on a number of factors, such as age, activity level, food quality, reproductive status and size. What's the easiest way to figure it out? Start with the manufacturer's recommended amount, and adjust it according to your dog's response. For example, if you feed the recommended amount for a few weeks and your Shih Tzu loses weight, increase the amount by 10 to 20 percent. If your dog gains weight, decrease the amount. It won't take long to determine the amount of food that keeps your little friend in optimal condition.

NUTRITION 101

All Shih Tzu (and every breed, for that matter) need proteins, carbohydrates, fats, vitamins and minerals for their optimal growth and health.

■ **Proteins** are used for growth and the repair of muscles, bones and other bodily tissues. They're also used for the production of antibodies, enzymes and hormones. All dogs need protein, but it's especially important for puppies because they grow so rapidly. Protein sources in dog food include various types of meats, meat meal, meat by-products, eggs and dairy products.

■ **Carbohydrates** are metabolized into glucose, the body's energy source, and they are available as sugars, starches and fiber.

• Sugars (simple carbohydrates) are not suitable nutrient sources for dogs.

Believe it or not, during your Shih Tzu's lifetime, you'll buy a few thousand pounds of dog food! Go to **DogChannel.com/Club-ShihTzu** and download a chart that outlines the cost of dog food.

- Starch — a preferred type of carbohydrate in dog food — is found in a variety of plant products. Starches must be cooked in order to be digested.
- Fiber (cellulose) — also a preferred type of carbohydrates in dog food — isn't digestible, but it helps the digestive tract function properly.

■ **Fats** are also required for energy and play an important role in skin and coat health, hormone production, nervous system function and vitamin transport. Fat increases the palatability and the calorie count, which can contribute to serious health problems, such as obesity, for puppies or dogs who are allowed to overindulge. Some foods contain added amounts of omega fatty acids such as docosohexaenoic acid, a compound that may enhance brain development and learning in Shih Tzu puppies but is not considered an essential nutrient by the Association of American Feed Control Officials (www.aafco.org). Fats used in dog foods include tallow, lard, poultry fat, fish and vegetable oils.

■ **Vitamins** and **minerals** participate in muscle and nerve function, bone growth, healing, metabolism and fluid balance. Especially important for your puppy are calcium, phosphorus and vitamin D, which must be supplied in the right balance to ensure proper bone and teeth development.

Just as your dog needs proper nutrition from his food, **water** is an essential nutrient, as well. Water keeps a dog's body properly hydrated and promotes normal body system functions. During housetraining, it is necessary to keep an eye on how much water your Shih Tzu is drinking, but once he is reliably trained, he should have access to clean, fresh water at all times, especially if you feed him dry food. Make sure that the dog's water bowl is clean, and change the water often.

CHECK THE LABEL

To help you get a feel for what you are feeding your dog, start by taking a look at the nutrition labels. Look for the words "complete and balanced." This tells you that the food meets specific nutritional requirements set by the AAFCO for either adults ("maintenance") or puppies and pregnant/lactating females ("growth and reproduction"). The label must state the group for which it is

Buying food isn't a guessing game. Read the labels to get the inside scoop.

Dogs of all ages love treats and table food, but these goodies can unbalance your Shih Tzu's diet and lead to a weight problem if you don't choose and feed them wisely. Table food, whether fed as a treat or as part of a meal, should not account for more than 10 percent of your dog's daily caloric intake. If you plan to give your Shih Tzu treats, be sure to include "treat calories" when calculating the daily food requirement, so you don't end up with a pudgy pup!

When shopping for packaged treats, look for ones that provide complete nutrition. They're basically dog food in a fun form. Choose crunchy goodies for chewing fun and dental health. Other ideas for tasty treats include:

✓ small chunks of cooked, lean meat
✓ dry dog food morsels
✓ cheese
✓ veggies (cooked, raw or frozen)
✓ breads, crackers or dry cereal
✓ unsalted, unbuttered, plain, popped popcorn

Some foods, however, can be dangerous or even deadly to your dog. The following can cause digestive upset (vomiting or diarrhea) or toxic reactions that could be fatal:

✗ **avocados:** can cause gastrointestinal irritation, with vomiting and diarrhea, if eaten in sufficient quantity

✗ **baby food:** may contain onion powder; does not provide balanced nutrition for a dog or pup

✗ **chocolate:** contains methylxanthines and theobromine, caffeine-like compounds that can cause vomiting, diarrhea, heart abnormalities, tremors, seizures and even death. Darker chocolates contain higher levels of the toxic compounds.

✗ **eggs, raw:** whites contain an enzyme that prevents uptake of biotin, a B vitamin; may contain salmonella

✗ **garlic (and related foods):** can cause gastrointestinal irritation and anemia if eaten in sufficient quantity

✗ **grapes/raisins:** can cause kidney failure if eaten in sufficient quantity (the toxic dose varies from dog to dog)

✗ **macadamia nuts:** can cause vomiting, weakness, lack of coordination and other problems

✗ **meat, raw:** may contain harmful bacteria such as salmonella or E. coli

✗ **milk:** can cause diarrhea in some puppies

✗ **onions (and related foods):** can cause gastro intestinal irritation and anemia if eaten in sufficient quantity

✗ **yeast bread dough:** can rise in the gastrointestinal tract, causing obstruction; produces alcohol as it rises

intended. If you're feeding a puppy, choose a "growth and reproduction" food.

The label also includes a nutritional analysis, which lists minimum protein, minimum fat, maximum fiber and maximum moisture content, as well as other information. (You won't find carbohydrate content because it's everything that isn't protein, fat, fiber and moisture.)

The nutritional analysis refers to crude protein and crude fat — amounts determined in the laboratory. This analysis is technically accurate, but it does not tell you anything about digestibility — how much of the particular nutrient your Shih Tzu can actually use. For information about digestibility, contact the manufacturer (check the label for a phone number and website).

Virtually all commercial puppy foods exceed the AAFCO's minimal requirements for protein and fat, the two nutrients most commonly evaluated when comparing foods. Protein levels in dry puppy foods usually range from about 26 to 30 percent;

for canned foods, the values are about 9 to 13 percent. The fat content of dry puppy foods is about 20 percent or more; for canned foods, it's 8 percent or more. Dry food values are larger than canned food values because dry food contains less water; the values are actually similar when compared on a dry matter basis.

Finally, check the ingredients on the label, listed in descending order by weight.

A healthy, shiny coat doesn't begin with an expensive conditioner; it begins with proper nutrition.

Feeding your dog is part of your daily routine. Take a break, and have some fun online and play "Feed the Shih Tzu," an exclusive game found only on **DogChannel.com/Club-ShihTzu** — just click on "Games."

How can you tell if your Shih Tzu is fit or fat? When you run your hands down your pal's sides from front to back, you should be able to easily feel her ribs. It's OK if you feel a little body fat (and, of course, a lot of hair), but you should not feel huge fat pads. You should also be able to feel your Shih Tzu's waist — an indentation behind the ribs.

Manufacturers are allowed to list separately different forms of a single ingredient (e.g., ground corn and corn gluten meal). The food may contain things like meat byproducts, meat and bone meal, and animal fat, which probably won't appeal to you but are nutritious and safe for your dog. Higher quality foods usually have meat or meat products at the top of the ingredient list, but you don't need to worry about grain products as long as the label indicates that the food is nutritionally complete. Dogs are omnivores (not carnivores, as commonly believed), so all balanced dog foods contain animal and plant ingredients.

STAGES OF LIFE

When selecting your dog's diet, three stages of development must be considered: the puppy stage, the adult stage and the senior stage.

Puppy Diets: Pups instinctively want to nurse, and a normal puppy will exhibit this behavior from just a few moments following birth. Puppies should be allowed to nurse for about the first six weeks, although from the third or fourth week, the breeder will begin to introduce small portions of suitable solid food. Most breeders like to introduce alternate milk and meat meals initially, building up to weaning time.

By the time puppies are 7, a maximum of 8, weeks old, they should be fully weaned and fed solely a proprietary puppy food. Selection of the most suitable, good-quality diet at this time is essential, for a puppy's fastest growth rate is during the first year of his life. Seek advice about your dog's food from your veterinarian. The frequency of meals will be reduced over time, and when a young dog has reached about 10 to 12 months of age, he should be switched to an adult diet.

Puppy and junior diets can be balanced for the needs of your Shih Tzu so, except in

Hypoglycemia (low blood sugar) is a potentially life-threatening problem for Shih Tzu and other toy breeds. The most common type of hypoglycemia occurs in puppies younger than four months of age. Puppies typically develop hypoglycemia after exercising vigorously, when they're stressed (such as during a trip to the veterinarian) or when they've gone too long without eating.

Toy breed puppies have various anatomical, physiological and behavioral factors that contribute to the development of hypoglycemia: small muscle mass and liver (where glucose is stored as glycogen, a large molecule made up of many glucose molecules), proportionately large brain (a major user of glucose) and high activity level. Immaturity of the body's systems at processing and storing glucose may also play a role.

Early symptoms — trembling, listlessness, incoordination and a dazed or confused demeanor — occur when the brain is deprived of glucose, its sole energy supply. If untreated, hypoglycemia can lead to seizures, collapse, loss of consciousness and death.

If your Shih Tzu develops symptoms of hypoglycemia, start treatment immediately. Wrap your little buddy in a towel or blanket to keep her warm (shivering makes the hypoglycemia worse). If your Shih Tzu is conscious, slowly dribble a little corn syrup or honey into her mouth or give her a dollop of high-calorie dietary-supplement paste (available from your veterinarian). Repeat after 10 minutes, if necessary.

Feed your Shih Tzu puppy as soon as he's alert enough to eat. If hypoglycemia causes your Shih Tzu to lose consciousness, rub the syrup or paste on her gums and tongue, then immediately take her to the veterinarian for further care. If your puppy is prone to developing hypoglycemia, you should feed her a high-quality nutritionally balanced food four to five times a day.

Healthy high-calorie snacks may help prevent hypoglycemia between meals. If possible, avoid subjecting your Shih Tzu puppy to circumstances that may elicit hypoglycemia, such as stressful situations or extended periods of vigorous activity. Most puppies outgrow hypoglycemia by the time they're 4 months old. Consult your veterinarian if your dog continues to have hypoglycemic episodes after this age.

certain circumstances, additional vitamins, minerals and proteins will not be required.

How many times a day does your Shih Tzu need to eat? Puppies — especially toy breeds — have small stomachs and high metabolic rates, so they need to eat several times a day in order to consume sufficient nutrients. If your puppy is younger than 3 months old, feed him four or five meals a day. When your little buddy is 3 to 5 months old, decrease the number of meals to three or four. At 6 months of age, most puppies can move to an adult schedule of two meals a day. If your Shih Tzu is prone to hypoglycemia (low blood sugar), a veterinarian may recommend more frequent meals.

Adult Diets: A dog is considered an adult when he has stopped growing. Rely on your veterinarian or canine dietary specialist to recommend an acceptable maintenance diet for your dog. Major dog food manufacturers specialize in this type of food, and smart owners must select the one best suited to their dogs' needs. Do not leave food out all day for "free-choice" feeding, as this freedom inevitably translates to inches around your dog's waist.

Senior Diets: As dogs get older, their metabolism changes. An older dog usually exercises less, moves more slowly and sleeps more. This change in lifestyle and physiological performance requires a change in diet. Because these changes take place slowly,

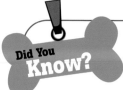

Did You Know?

Because semimoist food contains lots of sugar, it isn't a good selection for your Shih Tzu's main menu. However, it is great as a yummy snack for a toy dog. Try forming the food into little meatballs for a once-a-week treat! She'll love ya for it!

they might not be immediately recognized. These metabolic changes increase the tendency toward obesity, requiring an even more vigilant approach to feeding. Obesity in an older dog compounds the health problems that already accompany old age.

As your Shih Tzu gets older, few of his organs will function up to par. His kidneys will slow down, and his intestines will become less efficient. These age-related factors are best handled with a change in diet and feeding schedule to give smaller portions that are more easily digested.

There is no single best diet for every older dog. While many older dogs will do perfectly fine on light or senior diets, other dogs will do better on special premium diets such as lamb and rice. A smart owner will be prudent and sensitive to his or her senior Shih Tzu's diet, and this will help control other health complications that may arise with their old friend.

Be sure to add treats into your dog's daily caloric intake. If not, he could gain some extra pounds.

These delicious, dog-friendly recipes will have your furry friend smacking his lips and salivating for more. Just remember: Treats aren't meant to replace your dog's regular meals. Give your Shih Tzu snacks sparingly and continue to feed her nutritious, well-balanced meals.

Cheddar Squares

$1/3$ cup all-natural applesauce
$1/3$ cup low-fat cheddar cheese, shredded
$1/3$ cup water
2 cups unbleached white flour

In a medium bowl, mix all wet ingredients. In a large bowl, mix the flour and cheese. Slowly add the wet ingredients to the flour. Mix well. Pour batter into a greased 13x9x2-inch pan. Bake at 375-degrees Fahrenheit for 25 to 30 minutes. Bars are done when a toothpick inserted in the center and removed comes out clean. Cool and cut into bars. Makes about 54, 1 $1/2$-inch bars.

Peanut Butter Bites

3 tablespoons vegetable oil
$1/4$ cup smooth peanut butter, no salt or sugar
$1/4$ cup honey
1 $1/2$ teaspoons baking powder
2 eggs
2 cups whole wheat flour

In a large bowl, mix all ingredients until dough is firm. If the dough is too sticky, mix in a small amount of flour. Knead dough on a lightly floured surface until firm. Roll out dough until it is half an inch thick and cut with cookie cutters. Put cookies on a cookie sheet half an inch apart. Bake at 350-degrees Fahrenheit for 20 to 25 minutes. When done, cookies should be firm to the touch. Remove cookies from the oven, and leave cookies for one to two hours to harden. Makes about 40, 2-inch-long cookies.

The Shih Tzu was bred for royalty; his illustrious origins trace back to the emperors and royal court of China. So if one of these noble lion dogs is part of your family, he should get the royal treatment when it comes to taking care of his overall health and grooming needs.

This breed needs daily grooming. However, grooming is more than caring for your Shih Tzu's lovely coat; a basic grooming routine will help you monitor your dog's overall health and keep him in tiptop shape. Your Shih Tzu's grooming routine includes coat, teeth, eyes, ears and nail care. Each of these areas needs monitoring, and some require daily attention.

COAT CARE

In the show ring, the Shih Tzu has a beautiful, long, flowing coat that requires constant care. "Keeping a Shih Tzu in a long coat is time consuming because a lot of matting can occur," says breeder Barbara Pennington of Tualtin, Ore. So, if your Shih Tzu is bound for your couch instead of the show ring, consider keeping him in a puppy cut.

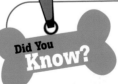

Did You Know?

Nail clipping can be tricky, so many dog owners leave the task to the professionals. However, if you walk your dog on concrete, you may not have to worry about it. The concrete acts like a nail file and may help keep the nails in check.

The Shih Tzu puppy cut is exactly that: a cut that looks like the coat he had as a 4- or 5-month-old puppy. "In a puppy cut, the hair should be one to two inches long and not shaved down to the skin," says breeder Pat Wagner of Knightsen, Calif.

The one part of the coat that doesn't get the puppy treatment is the topknot. This characteristic Shih Tzu fashion statement does more than look good; it keeps the hair out of your dog's nose, mouth and eyes.

The Shih Tzu is often referred to as "the chrysanthemum-faced dog" because the hair grows in all directions on his face. Although you can cut the hair on your dog's face, it grows quickly and in all directions, so you need to make sure that these short hairs aren't poking your Shih Tzu in the eye.

"The topknot is a hygienic way to keep the face area clean and tidy," Pennington says. A topknot can generally be worn once your puppy is 3 to 4 months old.

AT-HOME VS. THE SALON

You can learn to do a puppy cut yourself, but you'll need to invest in the appropriate equipment, such as clippers and how-to books and videos. Your breeder is also a resource when it comes to grooming, and he or she can usually help you learn how to administer a puppy cut at home.

Still, most owners opt for a trip to the groomers every four to six weeks for the full treatment — a puppy cut, brush, bath, nail clip, fresh topknot and possibly more, depending on the services offered by the groomers in your area.

Shih Tzu are the perfect size for a bath in a sink!

NOTABLE & QUOTABLE

After removing a tick, clean your dog's skin with hydrogen peroxide. If Lyme disease is common where you live, have your veterinarian test the tick. Tick preventative medication will discourage ticks from attaching and kill any that do.

— groomer Andrea Vilardi from West Paterson, N.J.

The Shih Tzu's beautiful coat can be a handful to care for if not attended to regularly. If you opt to visit a groomer to keep your Shih Tzu's coat neatly trimmed, you'll still need to do some weekly brushing to keep mats to a minimum. In general, you'll want to visit a groomer every four to six weeks.

Keep in mind that, puppies should not be trimmed before they are 5 months old.

BETTER BRUSHING

The Shih Tzu is a double-coated breed; an adult Shih Tzu has an outer coat and a cottony undercoat, which is what normally becomes matted. The texture of the coat changes when you Shih Tzu is about 9 to 12 months old. At this time they get lots of mats and can require daily brushing (because their adult coat tends to be a bit heavier), but once they get through this stage, the coat will form mats less often and care will be easier.

Even within the same breed, individual coat requirements can vary. The number of times per week you'll need to brush your Shih Tzu depends on how quickly he mats. You many need to brush him every day or every two to three days.

To properly brush your dog, you'll need a soft pin brush, or slicker brush, and a metal comb. You'll also want to combine a small amount of conditioner (especially made for dogs) with water in a spray bottle. Training a puppy to lie on his back while you rub his tummy is an important step in the brushing process, because mats tend to form on the underside of dogs in the armpits and toward their back legs.

To begin, place your dog on his back and lightly mist his coat with the conditioner-water solution to prevent any hair breakage. Use either a pin brush or slicker brush on the underside of your dog while he relaxes on his back.

Next, place your dog in a standing position and brush his sides, back and legs. When brushing his back, brush toward the tail; when brushing his sides and legs, brush toward the ground.

Finish with brushing the head area. After you've brushed your dog's coat, go back through it with a metal comb to make sure all the mats have been removed.

To bathe your Shih Tzu at home, use a shampoo and conditioner formulated for dogs. You can find these at pet-supply stores, dog shows or from online suppliers.

"Never bathe a dog with mats," Pennington says. "It's important to brush your dog thoroughly before a bath, because water will set the mats and make them extremely difficult, if not impossible, to brush out."

THE EYES HAVE IT

Tear stains tend to be a part of life with a Shih Tzu, they are a result of excessive tearing and are common in many breeds. The dampness created on the facial hair by this staining is the perfect breeding ground for bacterial and yeast growth. The most common is red yeast, which can cause reddish-brown facial stains and a slight odor.

The best way to prevent tear stains is by wiping your Shih Tzu's face daily. You can buy doggie eye wipes to clean under your dog's eyes, or you can go the homemade route. "If you're extremely careful, you can use a little bit of hydrogen peroxide on a cotton ball to gently wipe under your dog's eyes," Pennington says. Warner suggests another tip: "After you

Shih Tzu love to be brushed. It is a great bonding experience for dog and owner alike.

wipe the eyes, pat a little bit of cornstarch on the area to help keep it dry."

Again, be extremely careful when cleaning around your Shih Tzu's eyes, so you don't get hydrogen peroxide or cornstarch in them.

I'M ALL EARS

Like any breed with drop ears, Shih Tzu are prone to getting ear infections, so it's important to keep the ears clean. The shape, weight and length of the ear flap reduce air circulation within the ear canal. This creates a warm, dark, moist environment, which is the perfect breeding ground for bacterial and yeast infections.

Ear care isn't difficult; it just needs to be done regularly. Remember, you only need to clean the ears when they are dirty. Every dog is different, some may need weekly cleanings to keep their ears clean and fresh, while others might only need monthly care. In any case, check the condition of your Shih Tzu's ears on a weekly basis. The amount of dirt and debris you can see around his ears will determine how often they need to be cleaned.

To clean your dog's ears, you'll need a liquid ear cleaner and cotton balls. Several different brands of ear cleaner are available; check with your veterinarian for his or her recommendation.

To begin, lift the flap of your Shih Tzu's ear, so his ear canal is open and accessible. Place the opening of the cleaner into your dog's ear and gently squirt the liquid into his ear. Then, gently massage the base of his ear. If your dog wants to shake after the massage, let him.

JOIN OUR ONLINE Club Shih Tzu®

Every Shih Tzu should look dapper. What do you need to keep your dog looking his best? Go to Club Shih Tzu (**DogChannel.com/Club-ShihTzu**) and download a checklist of essential grooming equipment you and your toy dog will need.

Don't let the name fool you. A puppy cut looks great on adult Shih Tzu, too!

After the massage, use a cotton ball to remove any discharge or debris from around the inside of your dog's ear. Only clean the part of the ear that you can see. Do not dig inside the ear or try to go deep into the ear canal. Repeat on the other ear.

NEAT FEET

A groomer should trim your Shih Tzu's nails during a regular visit, but you may need to trim his nails between trips to the groomer, too. Generally, it's a good idea to trim nails on a weekly basis to keep them nice and short.

To trim nails at home, you'll need nail clippers (either a scissor- or guillotine-type) and styptic powder (a blood coagulant).

Each type of nail clipper works equally well, but most people find they have a definite preference for one style or the other.

At the center of each nail is its blood and nerve supply, called the quick. In white nails, you can identify the quick by its pink color, for black or dark nails, shine a light under your dog's nails to see the quick. Trim the nails as close to the quick as possible without cutting into it. Cutting the quick is painful for your dog and will result in a lot of bleeding.

If you accidentally cut the quick, apply styptic powder to the nail to stop the bleeding. It sometimes helps to have someone else hold your dog while you trim the nails.

Although some breeds can tolerate the

Grooming a Shih Tzu in show style requires a good groomer. If you prefer that classic look to the puppy cut, be prepared for a lot of work (which can be well-worth the effort!)

use of an electric nail grinder for nail trims, it isn't a good idea for your Shih Tzu. The long hair around your Shih Tzu's feet can easily become tangled in the circular motion of the grinder's head. When it comes to your Shih Tzu, stick with a good, manual nail clipper.

PEARLY WHITES

Eighty-five percent of all dogs will have some type of dental disease by age 3, so it's extremely important to keep your dog's teeth as plaque free as possible. Good dental care is vital to your dog's overall health.

Shih Tzu are extra challenging when it comes to dental care. "A Shih Tzu has small, rice-like teeth, a short nose and a small mouth with big fat lips," Wagner says. This can make it difficult to brush their teeth. "I give my Shih Tzu hard biscuits that are specially formulated to help keep teeth clean," she says. Try to clean your dog's teeth as often as possible — every day is best.

To brush your Shih Tzu's teeth, you'll need a toothbrush and toothpaste formulated for dogs, which usually comes in yummy flavors such as chicken and beef.

Did You Know?

The crunchiness of dry dog food helps keep teeth healthy and shiny by reducing plaque accumulation.

Don't use human toothpaste; it wasn't designed to be swallowed, and can cause an upset stomach. For your Shih Tzu's small mouth, try a human pediatric toothbrush. If using a toothbrush on your Shih Tzu just doesn't work, try pre-moistened canine dental wipes with a plaque inhibitor. The best time to start dental care is when your Shih Tzu is a puppy. As a puppy, he'll learn to accept dental care as a normal part of his grooming routine.

Introduce teeth cleaning slowly and gently. Start by letting your dog lick the toothpaste off your fingers, then slide your finger with the toothpaste into his mouth. Slowly work up to using a toothbrush or dental wipes throughout his mouth.

In addition to brushing at home, your Shih Tzu will need professional teeth cleanings performed by a veterinarian. Check with your vet to find out how often your dog's teeth need a professional cleaning and when to start.

TYING A TOPKNOT

The Shih Tzu's signature style is their dapper topknot. You can learn to do the topknot yourself or find a groomer to do it for you. Of course, nothing beats learning from experience, so once your Shih Tzu has enough hair for a topknot, ask your breeder for some hands-on topknot lessons.

Though you might think that a topknot is all for fashion and show, it actually serves an important purpose. A maintenance or casual topknot is worn to keep the face and head hair from falling into your Shih Tzu's eyes, nose and mouth. This natty grooming style will keep your Shih Tzu's face clean and hygienic — and looking fab!

To create a topknot, you'll need a good metal comb and small elastic bands that

won't break hair. You can purchase these bands at dog shows, pet-supply stores or even through an orthodontist (usually used for braces). Everyone has a different method for a creating a topknot, but the easiest will be the one you do for a puppy.

To create a simple puppy topknot, part and gather together the hair above the nose and between the eyes. Use a comb to part the hair between the eyes, from the inner corner of one eye to the inner corner of the other. Remember to work carefully around your Shih Tzu's eyes to avoid injury. For a puppy topknot, this hair is gathered and sectioned into an inverted V and secured with an elastic band. As your Shih Tzu gets older and his hair lengthens, add more sections to the topknot, eventually anchoring them all together and adding a bow.

For a casual topknot, follow these steps:

■ Like the puppy topknot, start by gathering the hair between the eyes from the inner corner of one eye to the inner corner of the other. Next, lift forward the hair you're holding, and make a part across the middle of the skull, then brush the first section forward. Tie an elastic band around this section.

■ Create another section by taking the comb through the hair toward the back of the

Is there anything cuter than a
freshly bathed Shih Tzu puppy?

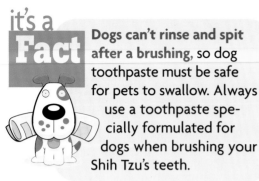
ear, across the head to the back of the other ear. Gather this section together and band it.

■ Tie a bow (if desired) on the first section, and then, join the two sections together with another band. Your Shih Tzu should look quite sharp now!

REWARD A JOB WELL DONE

Rewarding your pet for behaving during grooming is the best way to ensure stress-free grooming throughout his lifetime. Bathing energizes your dog, and using the time immediately after grooming as play time is the best way to reward your Shih Tzu for a job well done. Watching your clean, healthy toy tear from room to room in sheer joy is your reward for being a caring, and smart, owner.

Six Tips for Shih Tzu Care

1. Grooming tools can be scary to some dogs, so let yours see and sniff everything at the onset. Keep your beauty sessions short, too. Some dogs don't enjoy standing still for too long.
2. Look at your dog's eyes for any discharge, and her ears for inflammation, debris or foul odor. If you notice anything that doesn't look right, contact your veterinarian ASAP.
3. Choose a time to groom your dog when you don't have to rush and assemble all of the grooming tools before you begin. This way, you can focus on your dog's needs without having to stop in the middle of the session.
4. Start establishing a grooming routine the day after you bring her home. A regular schedule will make it easier to remember what touch-up tasks your dog needs.
5. Proper nail care will help with your dog's gait and spinal alignment. Nails that are too long can force a dog to walk improperly. Also, extra-long nails can snag and tear, causing painful injury to your Shih Tzu.
6. Good dental health prevents gum disease and early tooth loss. Brush your Shih Tzu's teeth daily and see a veterinarian annually.

Six Questions to Ask a Groomer

1. Do you cage dry? Are you willing to hand dry or air dry my pet?
2. What type of shampoo are you using? Is it tearless? If not, do you have a tearless variety available for use?
3. Will you restrain my dog if she acts up for nail clipping? What methods do you use for difficult dogs?
4. Are you familiar with the Shih Tzu breed? Do you have any references from other Shih Tzu owners?
5. Is the shop air-conditioned during hot weather?
6. Will my dog be getting brushed or just bathed?

TRAIN

You know the stereotype: The tiny dog nestled in the ample bosom of the wealthy dowager, snapping and snarling at all who come near. His feet never touch the ground, and no one other than his doting owner ever touches him.

What a shame. When given the opportunity, the Shih Tzu can be as much a dog as the best of them. It's easy to fall into the trap of thinking your Shih Tzu doesn't need training. He's so little; it's no big deal to just pick him up when you need to take him somewhere. But if you want him to be mentally and physically healthy — and to be a well-behaved member of society — you'll need to square your shoulders, and put your Shih Tzu back on the floor.

The increasing use of dog-friendly methods is a blessing to all dogs, and especially to toy breeds, which are most vulnerable to injury from heavy-handed training. It does not take much of a jerk on a choke chain to damage the trachea of a toy dog. Positive training techniques are basically the same for dogs of all sizes, but you'll encounter special challenges when you're training in miniature.

Did You Know? The prime period for socialization is short. Most behavior experts agree that positive experiences during the 10-week period between 4 and 14 weeks of age are vital to the development of a puppy who'll grow into an adult dog with a sound temperament.

LEARNING SOCIAL GRACES

Now that you have done all of the preparatory work and have helped your Shih Tzu get accustomed to his new home and family, it's time for a smart owner to have some fun! Socializing your tiny pup will give you the opportunity to show off your new friend, and your toy dog gets to reap the benefits of being an adorable little creature whom people will want to pet and, think is absolutely precious!

Besides getting to know his new family, your puppy should be exposed to other people, animals and situations. Of course, he must not come into close contact with dogs you don't know well until he has had all his vaccinations. This socialization process will help him become well-adjusted as he grows up and will make him less prone to being timid or fearful of the new things he will encounter.

Your pup's socialization began at the breeder's home, but now it is your responsibility to continue it. The socialization he receives up until 12 weeks is the most critical, as this is the time when he forms his impressions of the outside world, but they will still be plenty for you to teach him once you bring him home. The interaction he receives during puppyhood should be gentle and reassuring. Lack

SMART TIP!

If your toy dog refuses to sit with both haunches squarely beneath her and instead sits on one side or the other, she may have a physical reason for doing so. Discuss the habit with your veterinarian to be certain that your dog isn't suffering from some structural problem.

Socializing a puppy will make him confident about all the future encounters and situations he'll face as an adult.

of socialization can manifest itself as fear and aggression as the dog grows. The pup needs lots of human contact, affection, handling and exposure to other animals.

Once your Shih Tzu has received all of his necessary vaccinations, you can take him out and about (on his leash, of course). Walk him around the neighborhood, take him on errands, let people pet him and let him meet other dogs and pets. Expose your toy dog to different types of people — men, women, kids, babies, men with beards, teenagers with cell phones or riding skateboards, joggers, shoppers, someone in a wheelchair, a pregnant woman, etc. In addition, make sure your Shih Tzu explores different surfaces like sidewalks, gravel and a puddle. Positive experiences are key to building confidence. It's up to you to make sure your Shih Tzu safely discovers the world so he will be calm, confident and well-socialized.

It's important that you take the lead in all socialization experiences and never put your pup in a scary or potentially harmful situation. Be mindful of your Shih Tzu's limitations. Fifteen minutes at a public market is fine; two hours at a loud outdoor concert is too much. Meeting vaccinated, tolerant and gentle older dogs is great; meeting dogs you don't know isn't a great idea especially if they appear energetic, dominant or fearful. Control the situations in which you place your pup.

The best way to socialize your puppy to a new experience is to make him think it's the best thing ever. You can do this with a lot of happy talk, enthusiasm and, yes, food. To convince your puppy that almost any experience is a blast, always carry treats. Consider carrying two types — a bag of his puppy chow, which you can give him when introducing him to nonthreatening experiences, and a bag of high-value, mouth-watering treats to give him when introducing him to scarier experiences.

BASIC CUES

All Shih Tzu, regardless of your training and relationship goals, need to know at least five basic good-manner behaviors: sit, down, stay, come and heel. Here are tips for teaching your dog these important cues.

SIT: Every dog should learn how to sit.
- Hold a tasty treat at the end of your toy dog's nose.
- Move the treat over his head.
- When your Shih Tzu sits, click a clicker or say "Yes!"
- Feed your dog the treat.
- If your dog jumps up, hold the treat lower. If he backs up, back him into a corner and wait until he sits. Be patient. Keep your clicker handy, and click (or say "Yes!") and treat anytime he offers a sit.
- When he easily offers sits, say "sit" just before he offers, so he can make the association between the word and the behavior. Add the sit cue when you know you can get the behavior. Your dog doesn't

Don't keep training sessions going on for long stretches of time. Keep them short and sweet (with treats!), so your Shih Tzu will stay interested and motivated.

JOIN OUR ONLINE Club Shih Tzu®

With the proper training, your toy dog will be as well-behaved as she is adorable. One certification that all dogs should receive is the American Kennel Club Canine Good Citizen, which rewards dogs with good manners. Go to **DogChannel.com/Club-ShihTzu** and click on "Downloads" to get the 10 steps required for your dog to be a CGC.

Behaviors are best trained by breaking them down into their simplest components, teaching those and then linking them together to end up with the complete behavior. Keep treats small so you can reward many times without stuffing your Shih Tzu. Remember, don't bore your toy dog; avoid excessive repetition.

know what the word means until you repeatedly associate it with the appropriate behavior.

• When your Shih Tzu sits easily on cue, start using intermittent reinforcement by clicking some sits but not others. At first, click most sits and skip an occasional one (this is a high reinforcement rate). Gradually make your clicks more and more random.

DOWN: If your dog can sit, then he can learn to lie down.

◆ Have your Shih Tzu sit.

◆ Hold the treat in front of his nose. Move it down slowly, straight toward the floor (toward his toes). If he follows all the way down, click and treat.

◆ If he gets stuck, slowly move the treat down. Click and treat for small movements downward — moving his head a bit lower or inching one paw forward. Keep clicking and treating until your Shih Tzu is all the way down. This is called "shaping" —

rewarding small pieces of a behavior until your dog succeeds.

◆ If your dog stands as you move the treat toward the floor, have him sit and move the treat more slowly downward, shaping with clicks and treats for small movements down as long as he is sitting. If he stands, cheerfully say "Oops!" (which means "Sorry, no treat for that!"), have him sit and try again.

◆ If shaping isn't working, sit on the floor with your knee raised. Have your Shih Tzu sit next to you. Put your hand with the treat under your knee and lure him under your leg so that he lies down and crawls to follow the treat. Click and treat!

◆ When you can lure the down easily, add the verbal cue, wait a few seconds to let your dog think, then lure him down to show him the association. Repeat until he'll go down on the verbal cue. Then begin using intermittent reinforcement.

STAY: What good are sit and down cues if your dog doesn't stay?

▲ Start with your Shih Tzu in a sit or down position.

▲ Put the treat in front of your dog's nose and keep it there.

▲ Click and reward several times while he is in position, then release him with a cue that you will always use to tell him the stay is over. Common release cues are: "all done," "break," "free," "free dog," "at ease" and "OK."

▲ When your Shih Tzu will stay in a sit or down position while you click and treat, add your verbal stay cue. Say "stay," pause for a second or two, click and say "stay" again. Release.

▲ When your Shih Tzu is getting the idea, say "stay," whisk the treat out of sight behind your back, click and whisk the treat back. Be sure to get it all the way to his nose, so he does not jump up. Gradually increase the duration of the stay.

▲ When your Shih Tzu will stay for 15 to 20 seconds, add small distractions: shuffling your feet, moving your arms, small hops, etc. Increase distractions gradually. If he makes mistakes, you're adding too much, too fast.

▲ When he'll stay for 15 to 20 seconds with distractions, gradually add distance. Have your dog stay, take a half-step back, click, return and treat. When he'll stay with a half-step, tell him to stay, take a full step back, click and return. Always return to your dog to treat after you click, but before you release. If you always return, his stay

SMART TIP!

If you begin teaching the heel cue by taking long walks and letting the dog pull you along, she may misinterpret this action as an acceptable form of taking a walk. When you pull back on the leash to counteract her pulling, she will read that tug as a signal to pull even harder!

becomes strong. If you call him to you, his stay gets weaker due to his eagerness to come to you.

COME: A reliable recall — coming when called — can be a challenging behavior to teach. To teach this cue successfully, you need to install an automatic response to your "come" cue — one so automatic that your Shih Tzu doesn't even stop to think when he hears it, but will spin on his heels and charge to you at full speed.

If your Shih Tzu already ignores the word "come," pick a different cue, like "front" or "hugs." Say your cue and feed him a bit of scrumptious treat. Repeat this until your toy dog's eyes light up when he hears the cue. Now you're ready to start training.

With your Shih Tzu on a leash, run away several steps and cheerfully call out your charged cue. When he follows, click the clicker. Feed him a treat when he reaches you. For a more enthusiastic come, run away at full speed as you call him. When he follows at a gallop, click, stop running and give him a treat. The better your Shih Tzu gets at coming, the farther away he can be when you call .

Once your Shih Tzu understands the come cue, play with more people, each with a clicker and treats. Stand a short distance apart and take turns calling and running away. Click and treat in turn as he comes to each of you. Gradually increase the distance until he comes flying to each person from greater distances.

When you and your Shih Tzu are ready to practice in wide-open spaces, attach a long line — a 20- to 50-foot leash — to your dog, so you can gather up your Shih Tzu if a nearby temptation is too

much. Then, head to a practice area where there are less tempting distractions.

HEEL: Heeling means that your dog walks beside you without pulling. It takes time and patience on your part to succeed at teaching your dog that you will not proceed unless he is walking calmly beside you. Pulling out ahead on the leash is definitely not acceptable.

● Begin by holding the leash in your left hand as your Shih Tzu sits beside your left leg. Move the loop end of the leash to your right hand, but keep your left hand short on the leash so it keeps your dog close to you.

● Say "heel" and step forward on your left foot. Keep your Shih Tzu close to you and take three steps. Stop and have the dog sit next to you in what is called the heel position. Praise verbally, but do not touch your dog. Hesitate a moment and begin again with "heel," taking three steps and stopping, at which point the dog is told to sit again.

Your goal here is to have your Shih Tzu walk those three steps without pulling on the leash. Once he will walk calmly beside you for three steps without pulling, increase the number of steps you take to five. When he will walk politely beside you while you take five steps, you can increase the length of your walk to 10 steps. Keep increasing the length of your stroll until your toy dog will walk quietly beside you without pulling for as long as you want him to heel. When you stop heeling, indicate to the dog that the exercise is over by petting him and saying "OK, good dog." The "OK" is used as a release word, meaning that the exercise is finished, and he is free to relax.

● If you are dealing with a Shih Tzu who insists on pulling, simply put on your brakes and stand your ground until your Shih Tzu realizes that the two of you are not going anywhere until he is beside you and moving at your pace, not his. It may take some time just standing there to convince your dog that you are the leader, and you will be the one to decide on the direction and speed of your travel.

● Each time your dog looks up at you or slows down to give a slack leash between the two of you, quietly praise him and say, "Good heel. Good dog." Eventually, your Shih Tzu will begin to respond, and within a few days he will be walking politely beside you without pulling on the leash. At first, the training sessions should be kept short and very positive; soon your dog will be able to walk nicely with you for increasingly longer distances. Remember to give your dog free time and the opportunity to run and play when you have finished heel practice.

If you have an adult and a puppy, let the puppy watch the adult perform cues. He might learn by imitation.

If you want to make your dog happy, create a digging spot where she's allowed to disrupt the earth. Encourage her to dig there by burying bones and toys, and helping her dig them up. — Pat Miller, certified pet dog trainer and owner of Peaceable Paws dog-training facility in Hagerstown, Md.

Use high-value treats when you are trying to teach a very important cue.

TRAINING TIPS

If not properly socialized, managed and trained, even a well-bred Shih Tzu will exhibit undesirable behaviors such as jumping up, barking, chasing and chewing. You can prevent these annoying habits and help your Shih Tzu become the perfect dog you've wished for by following some basic training and behavior guidelines.

Use appropriately-sized equipment. Purchase collars and leashes to scale for your little one. A huge brass buckle is like an anchor for your Shih Tzu, and if it smacks him in the face once or twice, he won't be eager to train or go for walks with you. A harness may be a better choice for a Shih Tzu than a collar, to avoid any potential damage to the throat.

Move gently. Try to lighten your step and move with gentle purpose when training and interacting with your Shih Tzu. You probably outweigh your pup 20 to 30 times. Imagine strolling next to a 2,500-pound gargantuan towering over you. Now imagine that gargantuan stomping in heavy boots, barely missing your tiny self with each step. Tread lightly and wear soft-soled shoes.

Use teensy treats. With mid- to large-sized dogs, we feed pea-sized treats. With itty-bitty dogs you need to use rice-grain-sized treats. If your treats are too large your Shih Tzu will fill up in no time and your training sessions will be too short.

Be safe. Your dog depends on you to be his protector and defender. Don't ever let anyone — your trainer, groomer, veterinarian, friends, family — do anything to him that you aren't comfortable with, and don't let yourself be talked into doing anything against your better judgment. Although it's good for him to play with other dogs to be well-adjusted, larger dogs can and do present a significant threat to a toy dog's safety. More than one little dog has been killed in the jaws of a big dog. Err on the side of caution when choosing playmates for your Shih Tzu.

Think big. Don't let your Shih Tzu's diminutive size impede your training goals. If you want a well-socialized companion who accompanies you everywhere, he's your man. Toy dogs are often allowed places where their larger brothers aren't, so socialization is especially important for this breed.

THE THREE-STEP PROGRAM

Perhaps it's too late to give your dog consistency, training and management from the

SMART TIP!

Do not have long practice sessions with your Shih Tzu. She will become easily bored if you do. Also: Never practice when you are tired, ill, worried or in a negative mood. This will transmit to your Shih Tzu and may have an adverse effect on her performance.

start. Maybe he came from a toy dog rescue or a shelter, or you didn't realize the importance of these rules when he was a pup. He already may have learned some bad behaviors, perhaps they're even part of his genetic package. Many problems can be modified with ease using the following three-step process for changing an unwanted behavior.

STEP NO. 1: Visualize the behavior you want from your dog. If you simply try to stop your pup from doing something, you leave a behavior vacuum. You need to fill that vacuum with something, so your dog doesn't return to the same behavior or fill it with one that's even worse! If you're tired of your dog jumping up, decide what you'd prefer instead. A dog who greets people by sitting politely in front of them is a joy to own.

STEP NO. 2: Prevent your toy dog from being rewarded for the behavior you don't want. Management to the rescue! When your toy dog jumps up to greet you or get your attention, turn your back and step

NOTABLE & QUOTABLE

Sit on the floor to practice your dog's training exercises. It's less intimidating for her — and easier on your back. Alternatively, set her on a raised surface, such as a table-top covered with a blanket. Make sure she's comfortable and confident there — if not, go back to the floor. — Pat Miller, certified pet dog trainer and owner of the Peaceable Paws dog-training facility in Hagerstown, Md.

away to show him that jumping up no longer works.

STEP NO. 3: Generously reinforce the desired behavior. Remember, dogs repeat behaviors that reward them. If your Shih Tzu no longer gets attention for jumping and is heavily reinforced with attention and treats for sitting, he will offer sits instead of jumping, because sits get him what he wants.

COUNTER CONDITIONING

Behaviors that respond well to the three-step process are those where the dog does something in order to get good stuff. He jumps up to get attention. He countersurfs because he finds good stuff on the counters. He nips at your hands to get you to play with him.

The three steps don't work well when you're dealing with behaviors that are based in strong emotion, such as aggression and fear, or with hardwired behaviors such as chasing prey. With these, a smart owner can change the emotional or hardwired response through counter conditioning — programming a new emotional or automatic response to the stimulus by giving it a new association. Here's how you would counter condition a Shih Tzu who chases after skateboarders when you're walking him on a leash.

Yummy treats are great training motivators, but praise and petting are just as valuable. Mix and match to keep your Shih Tzu guessing!

1. Have a large supply of very high-value treats on hand, such as canned chicken.

2. Station yourself with your Shih Tzu on a leash at a location where skateboarders will pass by at a subthreshold distance "X" — that is, where your Shih Tzu alerts but doesn't lunge and bark.

3. Wait for a skateboarder. The instant your Shih Tzu notices the skateboarder, feed him bits of chicken, nonstop, until the skateboarder is gone.

4. Repeat many times until, when the skateboarder appears, your Shih Tzu looks at you with a big grin as if to say, "Yay! Where's my chicken?" This is a conditioned emotional response, or CER.

5. When you have a consistent CER at X, decrease the distance slightly, perhaps by 1 foot, and repeat until you consistently get the CER at this distance.

6. Continue decreasing the distance and obtaining a CER at each level, until a skateboarder zooming right past your Shih Tzu elicits the happy "Where's my chicken?" response. Now go back to distance X and add a second zooming skateboarder. Continue this process of gradual desensitization until your Shih Tzu doesn't turn a hair at a bevy of skateboarders.

LEAVE IT ALONE

Toy dogs enjoy eating, which makes it easy to train them using treats. But there's a downside to that gastronomic gusto — some Shih Tzu gobble down anything even remotely edible. This could include fresh food, rotten food, things that once were food and any item that's ever been in contact with food. So, if you don't want your Shih Tzu gulping trash, teach him to leave things alone when told.

Place a tempting tidbit on the floor and cover it with your hand (gloved against teeth, if necessary). Say your cue word ("Leave it" or "Nah"). Your dog might lick, nibble and paw your hand; don't give in or you'll be rewarding bad manners.

Wait until your dog moves away, then click or praise and give him a treat. Do not let your dog eat the temptation food that's on the floor, only the treats you give him. Repeat until your dog stops moving toward the food temptation.

Lift your hand momentarily, letting your dog see the temptation. Say the cue word. Be ready to protect the treat but instantly reward him if he resists temptation. Repeat, moving your hand farther away and waiting longer before clicking and rewarding.

Gradually increase the difficulty — practice in different locations, add new temptations, drop treats from standing height and drop several at a time and step away.

Remember to use your cue word, so your Shih Tzu will know what he's expected to do. Always reward good behavior! Rehearse this skill daily for a week. After that, you'll have enough real-life opportunities to practice.

BAD HABITS

Discipline — training one to act in accordance with rules — brings order to life. It is as simple as that. Without discipline, particularly in a group society, chaos reigns supreme and the group will eventually perish. Humans and canines are social animals and need some form of discipline in order to function effectively. Dogs need discipline in their lives in order to understand how their pack (you and other family members) functions and how they must act in order to survive.

Living with an untrained dog is a lot like owning a piano you don't know how to play; it's a nice object to look at but, it doesn't do much else for you. Now, begin taking piano lessons and suddenly the piano comes alive and brings forth magical sounds that set your heart singing and your body swaying.

The same is true with your Shih Tzu. Any dog is a big responsibility, and if not trained, may develop unacceptable behavior that annoy you or could even cause friction within the family.

Did You Know?

Anxiety can make a puppy miserable. Living in a world with scary monsters and suspected Shih Tzu-eaters roaming the streets has to be pretty nerve-wracking. The good news is that timid dogs are not doomed to be forever ruled by fear. Owners who understand a timid Shih Tzu's needs can help her build self-confidence and a more optimistic view of life.

To properly train a toy dog, a smart owner should consider enrolling tier Shih Tzu in an obedience class, where he can learn good manners as you learn how and why he behaves the way he does.

Suddenly, your dog will take on a new role in your life; he is smart, interesting, well-behaved and fun to be with. He demonstrates his bond of devotion to you daily. In other words, your Shih Tzu does wonders for your ego because he constantly reminds you that you are not only his leader, you are his hero!

Those involved with teaching dog obedience and counseling owners about their dogs' behavior have discovered some interesting facts about dog ownership. For example, training dogs when they are puppies results in the highest success rate in developing well-mannered and well-adjusted adult dogs. Training an older dog — from 6 months to 6 years of age — can produce almost equal results providing that a smart owner accepts the dog's slower rate of learning capability and is willing to work patiently to help the dog succeed by developing to his fullest potential. Unfortunately, many owners of untrained adult dogs lack the patience, so they do not persist until their dogs are successful at learning particular behaviors.

Training a puppy aged 12 to 16 weeks (20 weeks at the most) is like working with a dry sponge in a pool of water. The pup soaks up whatever you show him and constantly looks for more things to do and learn. At this early age, his body is not yet producing hormones, therein is the reason for such a high success rate. Without hormones, he is focused on his owners and not particularly interested in investigating other places, dogs, people, etc. You are his leader: his provider of food, water, shelter and security. He latches onto you and wants to stay close. He will usually follow you from room to room, will not let you out of his sight when you are outdoors with him and will respond in a similar manner to the people and animals you encounter. If you greet a friend warmly, he will be happy to greet the person as well. If, however, you are hesitant, even anxious, about the approach of a stranger, he will respond accordingly.

Once the puppy begins to produce hormones, his natural curiosity emerges and he begins to investigate the world around him. It is at this time when you may notice that the untrained dog begins to wander away from you and even ignore your cues to stay close.

There are usually classes within a reasonable distance of your home, but you also can do a lot to train your dog yourself. Whatever the circumstances, the key to successfully training your Shih Tzu without formal obedience classes lies within the pages of this book. This chapter is devoted to helping you train your Shih Tzu at home. If the recommended procedures are followed faithfully, you may expect positive results that will prove rewarding to you and your dog.

Whether your new companion is a puppy or a mature adult, the methods of teaching along with the techniques used in training,

NOTABLE & QUOTABLE

The best way to get through to dogs is through their stomach and mind — not the use of force. You have to play a mind game with them.

— *Sara Gregware, professional dog handler and trainer in Goshen, Conn.*

The golden rule of dog training is simple. For each "question" (cue), there is only one correct "answer" (reaction). One cue equals one reaction. Keep practicing the cue until your dog reacts correctly without hesitation. Be repetitive but not monotonous. Dogs get bored just as people do; a bored dog will not be focused on the lesson.

basic behaviors, are the same. After all, no dog — whether puppy or adult — likes harsh or inhumane methods. All creatures, however, respond favorably to gentle, motivational methods combined with sincere praise.

The following behavioral problems are the ones that dog owners encounter most. Every dog and situation is unique. Because behavioral abnormalities are the primary reason owners abandon their pets, we hope that you will make a valiant effort to train your Shih Tzu from the start.

NIP NIPPING

As puppies start to teethe, they feel the need to sink their teeth into everything; unfortunately, that includes your fingers, arms, hair, toes, whatever happens to be available. You may find this behavior cute for about the first five seconds — until you feel just how sharp those puppy teeth are.

Nipping is something you want to discourage immediately and consistently with a firm "No!" (or whatever number of firm "Nos" it takes for your dog to understand that you

mean business) and replace your finger with an appropriate chew toy.

STOP THAT WHINING

A puppy will often cry, whine, whimper, howl or make some type of commotion when left alone. This is basically his way of calling out for attention, to make sure you know he is there and that you have not forgotten about him. He feels insecure when he is left alone; when you are out of the house and he is in his crate or when you are in another part of the house and he cannot see you. The noise he is making is an expression of the anxiety he feels at being alone, so he needs to be taught that being alone is OK. You are not actually training your dog to stop making noise, you are training him to feel comfortable when he is alone and thus removing the need to make the noise.

This is where the crate with a cozy blanket and a toy comes in handy. You want to know that your puppy is safe when you are not there to supervise, and you know that he will be safe in his crate rather than roaming about the house. In order for the pup to stay in his crate without making a fuss, he needs to be comfortable there. On that note, it is extremely important that his crate is never used as a form of punishment, or your Shih Tzu will develop a negative association with his crate.

Acclimate your pup to his crate in short, gradually increasing intervals of time in which you put him in the crate with a treat and stay in the room with him. If he cries or makes a fuss, don't go to him, but stay in his sight. Eventually, he will realize that staying in his crate is OK without your help, and it will not be so traumatic for him when you are away. You may want to leave the radio on softly when you leave the house; the sound of human voices can be comforting to him.

CHEW ON THIS

The national canine pastime is chewing! Every dog loves to sink his "canines" into a tasty bone, but most anything will do. Dogs need to chew to massage their gums, to make their new teeth feel better and to exercise their jaws. This is a natural behavior deeply embedded in all things canine.

Did You Know? Dogs do not understand our language. They can be trained, however, to react to a certain sound, at a certain volume. Never use your dog's name during a reprimand, as she might come to associate it with a bad thing!

Our role as owners is not to stop our dog from chewing, but to redirect him to appropriate, chew-worthy objects. Be an informed owner and purchase proper chew toys for your toy dog, like strong nylon bones made for mouthy dogs. Be sure that the toys are safe and durable, because your dog's safety is at risk.

The best answer is prevention: That is, put your shoes, handbags and other tasty objects in their proper places (out of the reach of the canine mouth). Direct puppies to their toys whenever you see them tasting the furniture legs or the leg of your pants. Make a noise to attract your Shih Tzu's attention and immediately escort him to his chew toy and engage him with the toy for at least four minutes, praising and encouraging him all the while.

NO MORE JUMPING

Jumping up is a dog's friendly way of saying hello! Some owners don't mind when their dog jumps up, which is fine for them. The problem arises when guests arrive and your dog greets them in the same manner — whether they like it or not! However friendly the greeting may be, the chances are that your visitors will not appreciate your dog's enthusiasm. The dog will not be able to distinguish between whom he can jump upon and whom he cannot. Therefore, it is probably best to discourage this behavior entirely.

Pick a cue such as "off" (avoid using "down" because you will use that for your dog to lie down) and tell him "off" when he jumps up. Place him on the ground on all fours and have him sit, praising him the whole time. Always lavish him with praise and petting when he is in the sit position. That way you are still giving him a warm affectionate greeting, because you are as pleased to see him as he is to see you!

Your Shih Tzu may howl, whine or otherwise vocalize her displeasure at your leaving the house and her being left alone. This is a normal case of separation anxiety, but there are things that can be done to eliminate this problem. Your dog needs to learn that she will be fine on her own for a while and that she will not wither away if she isn't attended to every minute of the day.

In fact, constant attention can lead to separation anxiety. If you are endlessly coddling and cuddling your Shih Tzu, she will come to expect this behavior from you all of the time, and it will be more traumatic for her when you are not there.

To help minimize separation anxiety, make your entrances and exits as low-key as possible. Do not give your Shih Tzu a long, drawn-out goodbye and do not lavish her with hugs and kisses when you return. This will only make her miss you more when you are away. Another thing you can try is to give your dog a treat when you leave; this will keep her occupied, it will keep her mind off the fact that you just left and it will help her associate your leaving with a pleasant experience.

You may have to acclimate your Shih Tzu to being left alone in intervals, much like when you introduced her to her crate. Of course, when your dog starts whimpering as you approach the door, your first instinct will be to run to her and comfort her, but don't do it! Eventually, she will adjust and be just fine if you take it in small steps. Her anxiety stems from being placed in an unfamiliar situation; by familiarizing her with being alone she will learn that she is OK.

When your Shih Tzu is alone in the house, confine her in her crate or a designated dog-proof area. This should be the area where your Shih Tzu sleeps, so she will already feel comfortable there and more at ease when she is left alone during the day while you go to work or run errands. This is just one of the many examples in which a crate is an invaluable tool for you and your Shih Tzu, and reinforces why your toy dog should view her crate as a happy place of her own.

UNWANTED BARKING MUST GO

Barking is a dog's way of talking. It can be somewhat frustrating because it is not easy to tell what your dog means by his bark: Is he excited, happy, frightened, angry? Whatever it is that your dog is trying to say, he should not be punished for barking. It is only when the barking becomes excessive and a bad habit, that the behavior needs to be modified.

If an intruder came into your home in the middle of the night and your Shih Tzu barked a warning, wouldn't you be pleased? You would probably deem your dog a hero, a wonderful guardian and protector of the home. On the other hand, if a friend drops by unexpectedly and rings the doorbell and is greeted with a sudden sharp bark, you would probably be annoyed at your dog. Isn't it just the same behavior? Your dog doesn't know any better — unless he sees who is at the door and it is someone he is familiar with and will bark as a means of signaling to you that his (and your) territory is being threatened.

While your friend is not posing a threat, it's all the same to your Shih Tzu. Barking is his way of letting you know there is an intruder, whether friend or foe, on your property. This type of barking is instinctive and should not be discouraged.

Excessive habitual barking, however, is a problem that should be corrected early. As your Shih Tzu grows up, you will be able to tell when his barking is purposeful and when it is for no reason. You will become able to distinguish his different barks and their associations. For example, a Shih Tzu's bark will differ when someone is approaching the door from when he is excited to see you. It is similar to a person's tone of voice, except that a dog has to rely totally on tone of voice because he does not have the benefit of using words. An incessant barker will be evident at an early age.

There are some things that encourage a dog to bark. For example, if your dog barks nonstop for a few minutes and you give him a treat to quiet him, he will believe that you are rewarding him for barking. He will associate barking with getting a treat and will keep doing it until he is rewarded.

FOOD STEALING AND BEGGING

Is your dog devising ways to steal food? If so, you must answer these questions: Is your Shih Tzu really hungry? Why is there food on the coffee table? Face it, some dogs are more food-motivated than others; some dogs are totally obsessed by a slab of brisket and can only think of their next meal. Food stealing is terrific fun and always yields a great reward — food, glorious food!

The owner's goal, therefore, is to make the reward less rewarding, even startling! Plant a shaker can (an empty can filled with coins and covered with a lid) on the table so that it catches your pooch off-guard. There are other devices available that will surprise your dog when he is looking for a mid-afternoon snack. Such remote-control devices, though not the first choice of some trainers, allow the correction to come from the object instead of the owner. These devices are also useful to keep the snacking hound from napping on furniture.

SMART TIP!

Do not carry your puppy to her potty area. Lead her there on a leash, or better yet, encourage her to follow you to the spot. If you start carrying her, you might end up doing this routine for a long time and your Shih Tzu will have the satisfaction of having trained *you*.

Stage false departures. Pick up your car keys and put on your coat, then put them away and go about your routine. Do this several times a day, ignoring your dog while you do it. Soon her reaction to these triggers will decrease.

— *September Morn, a dog trainer and behavior specialist in Bellingham, Wash.*

Just like food stealing, begging is a favorite pastime of hungry puppies with that same food reward! Dogs quickly learn that humans love that feed-me pose and that their selfish owners keep the "good food" for themselves. Why would humans dine on kibble when they can cook up sausages and kielbasa? Begging is a conditioned response related to a specific stimulus, time and place. The sounds of the kitchen, cans and bottles opening, crinkling bags and the smell of food being prepared will excite the chowhound and soon the paws will be in the air!

Here is the solution to stop this behavior: Never give in to a beggar, no matter how cute or desperate! You are rewarding your dog for sitting pretty, jumping up, whining and rubbing his nose into you by giving him that glorious food reward. By ignoring the

dog, you will (eventually) force the behavior into extinction. Note that this behavior will likely get worse before it disappears, so be sure there aren't any softies in the family who will give in to your dog when he whimpers, "Pretty please."

DIG THIS

Digging, which is seen as a destructive behavior to humans, is actually quite a natural behavior in dogs and their desire to dig can be irrepressible and frustrating to owners. When digging occurs in your yard, it is actually a normal behavior redirected into something your dog can do in his everyday life. In the wild, a dog would be actively seeking food, making his own shelter, etc. He would be using his paws in a purposeful manner for his survival. Because you provide him with food and shelter, he has no need to use his paws for these purposes, and so the energy that he would be using may manifest itself in the form of little holes all over your yard and flower beds.

Perhaps your dog is digging as a reaction to boredom — it is somewhat similar to someone eating a whole bag of chips in front of the TV — because they are there and there is nothing better to do! Basically, the answer is to provide your dog with adequate play and exercise so that his mind and paws are occupied, and so that he feels as if he is doing something useful.

Of course, digging is easiest to control if it is stopped as soon as possible, but it is often hard to catch a dog in the act. If your dog is a compulsive digger and is not easily distracted by other activities, you can designate an area on your property where it is OK for him to dig. If you catch him digging in an off-limits area of the yard, immediately bring him to the approved area and praise him for digging there. Keep a close eye on him so you can catch him in the act; that is the only way to make him understand what is permitted and what is not. If you take him to a hole he dug an hour ago and tell him "No," he will understand that you are not fond of holes, dirt or uprooted flowers. If you catch him while he is deep in your tulips, that is when he will get your message.

POOP ALERT!

Humans find eating feces, aka *coprophagia*, one of the most disgusting behaviors that their dog could engage in; yet to your dog, it is perfectly normal. Vets have found that diets containing relatively low levels of fiber and high levels of starch, increase the incidence of coprophagia. Therefore, high-fiber diets may decrease the likelihood of dogs eating feces. To discourage this behavior, feed him a proper amount of food that is complete and balanced. If changes in his diet do not seem to work, and no medical cause can be found, you will have to modify the behavior through environmental control before it becomes a habit.

There are some tricks you can try to deter coprophagia in your dog, such as adding an unsavory substance to the feces to makes it unpalatable, or adding something to your dog's food which will make the feces taste unpleasant after it passes through your dog. The best way to prevent your dog from eating his stool is simply to make it unavailable; clean up after he eliminates and remove any stool from the yard. If it is not there, your Shih Tzu cannot eat it.

Never reprimand your dog for stool eating, as this rarely impresses him. Vets recommend distracting your dog while he is in the act of eating stool. Another option is to muzzle him when he is relieving himself in the yard; this usually is effective within 30 to 60 days. Coprophagia is most frequently seen in

Did You Know?

Some natural remedies for separation anxiety are reputed to have calming effects, but check with your vet before use. Flower essence remedies are water-based extracts of different plants, which are stabilized and preserved with alcohol. A human dose is only a few drops, so seek advice from a natural healing practitioner on proper dosage for your Shih Tzu.

pups 6 to 12 months of age, and usually disappears around the dog's first birthday.

LEASH PULLING

There are actually two types of loose-leash walking. One is "heeling," where the dog is on your left, looking up at you. The other is when your dog can be anywhere as long as the leash is loose. Both styles are fine, and both have their uses. Loose-leash walking is great for trail and potty walks. Heeling is great when you need to get your dog's attention to navigate a narrow spot or pass distractions.

A harness is great for walking a toy dog. Let's face it, small doesn't mean slow. Those tiny little legs are fast! And with that momentum comes jarring whiplash or possible neck or spinal damage if they hit the end of the leash at top speed. Harnesses help avoid these potential problems because they take the pressure off your dog's neck.

Use a long leash that is 15 feet or longer; that way you aren't forcing your dog to walk next to you. It is very important to give your dog the choice to stay with you (or not) but heavily reinforce the correct choice.

Arm yourself with a harness, a long leash

SMART TIP! It's a good idea to enroll in **an obedience class** if one is available in your area. Many areas have dog clubs that offer basic obedience training as well as preparatory classes for obedience competition. There are also local dog trainers who offer similar classes.

and a lot of tiny treats, good stuff like bits of cooked chicken, hot dog or small pieces of cheese. Although the same old dry biscuit may work as a treat in your kitchen, you don't need loose-leash walking in there. Your dog's paycheck has to be better outside to compete with the outdoors and the temptations they hold.

Before you start, you will need to teach your dog a marker signal — something that tells him when he did a behavior correctly at the exact instant he did it. You can use a clicker or the word "yes." Either click or say your word and instantly give him a treat. Repeat a few minutes per session, a few times per day for about two to three days. By that time he should know that the click or special word means a treat is coming.

Be sure to vary your reinforcement type. "Treat" doesn't have to always be food; you can use belly rubs, head pats, play, toys — whatever your dog likes.

Practice the following steps in many different kinds of locations; start with low-level distractions and gradually increase the intensity.

STEP 1 — PLAY: The first step to teaching loose-leash walking is to simply play with your dog. Fake left and right, race around and every few seconds, click him for staying with you and give him a few treats. Repeat for a few minutes per session, a few times per day. Once your dog realizes how much fun it is to be glued to you and you couldn't get rid of him if you tried, you are ready for the next move.

STEP 2 — BACK UP: While playing, start to walk backward, click as he follows you and give him a treat. Change direction frequently and every now and then, go back to play mode; this will encourage your dog to stay with you because you are being more fun. Gradually reduce the play and increase the backing up.

STEP 3 — PIVOT: Place the leash in your right hand and hold the treats in your left. If you reach around with your right hand to feed him on your left side, he will trip you in his attempt to get to your right side. Once your dog is a pro at back-ups, pivot (turn in place to your right) so he is on your left. Click and give him a few treats for each step he is still with you. Then, click and treat when he is looking up at you.

Slowly but surely, you can reduce the amount of treats for longer loose-leash walking. Once your dog is staying next to you on a regular basis, you can name this new behavior. The most common words are "heel," "with me" or "strut."

STEP 4 — CHECK IN: Go for a long walk. Let your dog sniff to his heart's content. When he happens to look back at you, click and jackpot! (Tons of tiny treats, all fed one treat at a time). Release him with a verbal "OK," and continue on your walk. Keep your eyes glued to him; each and every time he "checks in," click and jackpot. You should find that within a very short time, he'll stay right by your side. Click and feed him (and use those other reinforcers) when he is staying next to you. You can name this behavior "let's go," "let's walk" or anything you wish.

STEP 5 — MIX IT UP: Now that your dog knows how to heel and walk on a loose leash, mix it up. As you are walking, ask your

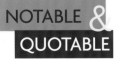 *The purpose of puppy classes is for puppies to learn how to
learn. The pups get the training along the way, but the
training is almost secondary.*
— *professional trainer Peggy Shunick Duezabou of Helena, Mont.*

dog to heel and see if he'll move into the heel position. If he does, click and treat (a lot!). Continue to click and treat for a few steps and then release him to continue on with his loose-leash walk. Periodically call him back to you to heel and then let him go again. Pretty soon you'll have a dog who loves to walk on a loose-leash and you will be the envy of all your neighbors — especially those who thought toy dogs couldn't be trained!

SEXUAL BEHAVIOR

Dogs exhibit certain sexual behaviors that may have influenced your choosing a male or female when you purchased your Shih Tzu. Spaying or neutering will eliminate most of these behaviors, but if you are purchasing a dog who you wish to show or breed, you should be aware of what you will have to deal with during the dog's life.

Females usually have two estruses (heat cyle) per year, each cycle lasting about three weeks. These are the only times she will mate, and she usually will not allow this until the second week. If she is not bred during the heat cycle, it is not uncommon for her to experience a false pregnancy, in which her mammary glands swell and she exhibits maternal tendencies toward her toys.

Owners must recognize that mounting, a common behavior, is not merely a sexual expression but also a way of displaying dominance. Be consistent and persistent, and you will find that you can "move mounters."

CAT INTRODUCTIONS

Cats are the pet most likely to arouse your puppy's interest. Besides all the other reasons you shouldn't let your puppy have run of the house, your cat is yet another. This is your cat's house, and cats are very territorial. Having a puppy invade your cat's territory isn't going to make things easier. When you

do start letting your puppy see more of the house, keep him on a leash and don't let him get into the cat's special places.

Your puppy is likely to want to play with your cat, and your cat is likely to not find this one bit amusing. If the puppy rushes at the cat, or even sniffs too brazenly, the pup is likely to get a swat in the face with some sharp claws. Although that may quickly teach him the hazards of cat chasing, it does so with the risk of a scratched eye. And if the cat runs, that's so rewarding to the puppy that he's likely to do it again.

Your best bet is to train both pets to coexist, and the best way to do that at first is to keep one in a crate while you train the other. Then take turns and have them trade places. Feed them next to each other or reward them with special treats for ignoring one another. Don't rush. You have years for them to be buddies, but you can sabotage it in days if you let things get out of hand.

Some older cats will remain snooty. You'll need to protect your puppy if your cat is the attacks, but don't let your cat win by removing your puppy from the room. When your cat is the one with the bad manners, he is the one who should leave the room. You don't want him to learn that beating up your puppy gets rid of the little trespasser.

Don't force your cat and Shih Tzu to be together if they don't want to. They will eventually work out what is a comfortable distance for each of them. Many cats and dogs grow to be close pals, while others prefer to look at each other from afar. The younger both are when you bring them home, the better the chance of them becoming fast, and furry, friends.

Don't turn all your pets loose on your new puppy all at once. Schedule "meetings" with each pet to help get the new relationship off on even ground.

Your Shih Tzu may look like little more than a miniscule, movable ball of fur with bright, shiny eyes, but don't let his small size fool you. There's a whole lot of energy in this toy that needs some fun and excitement.

EXERCISE OPTIONS

All dogs need exercise to keep them physically and mentally healthy. An inactive dog is an unfit dog, with the accompanying risk of joint strain or torn ligaments. Inactive dogs are also prone to mischief — and may do anything to relieve their boredom. This often leads to behavioral problems, such as chewing or barking. Regular daily exercise, such as daily walks and short play sessions, will help keep your Shih Tzu slim, trim and happy.

Provide your Shih Tzu with interactive play that stimulates his mind and body. It's a good idea to have a daily period of one-on-one playtime, especially with a puppy or young dog. Continue this type of interaction throughout your dog's life, and you will build a lasting bond. Even seniors who are slowing down a bit need the stimulation that activity provides.

If your Shih Tzu is older or overweight, consult your veterinarian about how much and what type of exercise he needs. Usually,

Did You Know? The Fédération Internationale Cynologique is the world kennel club that governs dog shows around the world.

Before You Begin

Because of the physical demands of dog sports, a Shih Tzu pup should not officially begin training until she is done growing. That doesn't mean that you can't begin socializing her to sports, though. Talk to your vet about what age is appropriate to begin more intense training.

a 10- to 15-minute walk once a day is a good start. As the pounds start to drop off, your dog's energy level will rise, and you can increase his amount of daily exercise.

Whether a dog is trained in a structured class or alone with his owner at home, there also are many sporting activities that can bring fun and rewards to owner and dog once they have mastered basic training techniques.

OBEDIENCE TRIALS

Obedience trials in the United States started in the early 1930s, when organized obedience training was developed to demonstrate how well a dog and his owner could work together. The pioneer of obedience trials was Helen Whitehouse Walker, a Standard Poodle fancier, who designed a series of exercises after the Associated Sheep, Police and Army Dog Society of Great Britain. Since then, obedience trials have grown by leaps and bounds, and today more than 2,000 trials are held in the United States every year, with more than 100,000 dogs competing.

Any registered American Kennel Club or United Kennel Club dog can enter an obedience trial for the club in which he is registered, regardless of conformational disqualifications or neutering.

Obedience trials are divided into three levels of progressive difficulty. At the Novice level, dogs compete for the title of Companion Dog; at the Open (intermediate) level, dogs compete for a Companion Dog Excellent title; and at the Advanced level, dogs compete for a Utility Dog title. Classes are subdivided into "A" (for beginners) and "B" (for more experienced handlers). A perfect score at any level is 200, and a dog must score 170 or better to earn a "leg," three of which are needed to earn the title. To earn points, the dog must score more than 50 percent of the available points in each exercise; the possible points range from 20 to 40. Once a dog has earned the UD title, he can compete with other proven obedience dogs for the coveted title of Utility Dog Excellent, which requires that a dog win "legs" in 10 shows.

In 1977, the AKC established a new title called the Obedience Trial Champion. Utility Dogs who earn legs in Open B and Utility B trials earn points toward earning the Obedience Trial Champion title. To become an OTCh., a dog is required to earn 100 points, which requires three first place wins in the Open B and Utility trials under three different judges.

The Grand Prix of obedience trials, the AKC National Obedience Invitational, gives qualifying Utility Dogs the chance to win the newest and highest title: National Obedience Champion. Only the top 25 ranked obedience dogs, plus any dog ranked in the top three in his breed, are allowed to compete.

AGILITY TRIALS

Agility is one of the most popular dog sports out there. Training your Shih Tzu in agility will boost his confidence and teach him to focus on you.

In agility competition, a dog and his handler move through a prescribed course,

Shih Tzu are indoor dogs, yes. But that doesn't mean they don't like to go outside from time to time for some fun and exercise.

maneuvering through a series of obstacles that may include jumps, tunnels, a dog walk, an A-frame, a seesaw, a pause table and weave poles. Dogs who run through a course without refusing any obstacles, going off course or knocking down any bars, all within a set time, get a qualifying score. Dogs with a certain number of qualifying scores in their given division (Novice, Open, Excellent and Mach, at AKC trials) earn an agility title.

Several different organizations recognize agility events. AKC-sanctioned agility events are the most common. The United States Dog Agility Association also sanctions agility trials, as does the United Kennel Club. The rules are different for each of these organizations, but the principles are the same.

When your Shih Tzu starts his agility training, he will begin by learning to navigate through each individual obstacle while on leash, as you guide him. Eventually, you will steer him through a few obstacles in a row, one after another. Once he catches on that this is how agility works, he can run a short course off leash. One day, you'll see the light go on in your Shih Tzu's eyes as he figures out that he should look to you for guidance as he runs through the agility course. Your job will be to tell him which obstacles to take next, using your voice and body as signals.

RALLY BEHIND RALLY

Rally is a sport that combines competition obedience with elements of agility but is less demanding than either one of these activities. Rally was designed with the average dog owner in mind, and is easier than many other sporting activities since it requires less formal and rigorous training.

At a rally event, dogs and handlers move through 10 to 20 different stations, depend-

ing on the level of competition. The stations are marked by numbered signs, which tell the handler the exercise to be performed at each station. The exercises vary from making different types of turns to changing pace.

Dogs can earn rally titles as they get better at the sport and move through the differ-

Did You Know? **Agility was initially designed for medium-sized breeds,** so it's not surprising that some obstacles present special challenges for diminutive dogs. The teeter-totter is probably the scariest and most difficult obstacle, because it tips and sinks under the dog, then hits the ground with a bang. That drop and sudden stop can be uncomfortable and can even bounce off a small dog. The plank end, hitting the ground and making a startling "bang," also distracts many small dogs.

ent levels. The titles to strive for are Rally Novice, Rally Advanced, Rally Excellent and Rally Advanced Excellent.

To get your Shih Tzu prepared for a rally competition, teach him basic obedience, for starters. Your dog must know the five basic obedience cues — sit, down, stay, come and heel — and perform them well before he's ready for rally. Next, enroll your dog in a rally class. Although he must be at least 6 months of age to compete in rally, you can start training long before his 6-month birthday.

FLYBALL

In the canine relay race of flyball, four straight-line hurdles lead to a box that ejects a tennis ball after impact on the release pedal. Hurdles are set at a height appropriate for the shortest dog on a team of four. Ideally, each dog leaps the hurdles, runs to the box, jumps on the pedal, catches the tennis ball in his mouth and repeats his path back to the waiting handler, cueing the next dog's release.

Flyball training may be difficult to find in some areas, though training clubs and private trainers certainly warrant an inquiring phone call. Should this route prove fruit-

less, purchase flyball equipment and start your own team!

MUSICAL FREESTYLE

A stunning combination of obedience, tricks and dance, freestyle is the perfect venue for those possessing an artistic flair. Set within a large, open ring, a handler and his dog perform a personally choreographed routine in rhythm to their choice of music. A typical presentation might find a dog weaving between the handler's legs as he or she is walking, spinning in place, doing leg kicks and other imaginative moves. Creative handler costumes and fancy dog collars often complete the picture.

Most participants agree that dogs display preferences in music, responding happily to tunes they like while ignoring those they don't. Deborah Wheeler of Gilmanton, N.H., says her Shih Tzu, Cain, enjoys musical freestyle training. "He's a happy little dog that loves to perform," she says.

If you're worried and self-conscious about your own dance skills, keep in mind that self-choreography allows you to focus on your team's special talents.

Find the ham in your little Shih Tzu at a local training facility or private trainer. Alternatively, contact the sport's host organizations, the Canine Freestyle Federation and the World Canine Freestyle Organization for information about getting your start in this exciting activity.

SHOW DOGS

When you purchase your Shih Tzu puppy, make it clear to the breeder whether you want one just as a lovable companion and pet, or if you're seeking a Shih Tzu with show prospects. No reputable breeder will sell you a puppy and tell you the dog will definitely be show quality because so much

SMART TIP!

Safety is another agility challenge for a toy dog. Contact obstacles, such as the teeter, dogwalk and A-frame, place dogs 2 to 6 feet off the ground. A fall from that height can injure any dog, and for a toy breed, it's a proportionally longer fall. When first training on contact obstacles, have a spotter on the opposite side of them if possible, in case your dog loses her balance.

After you run your dog at your first flyball tournament, you're hooked! With the Shih Tzu being such a social and entertaining breed, my dog thought that flyball sessions were just big parties and that he was the host. I had to use high-value treats — something so good he would do anything for them.

— flyball competitor Julie Wheeler of Wichita, Kan., talking about her Shih Tzu, Indy

it's a Fact

The Teacup Dogs Agility Association was formed to provide a competition venue for small dogs. Dogs of any breed or mix are welcomed in TDAA competitions — as long as they're not taller than 17 inches at the shoulder. Visit www.k9tdaa.com for more information.

can change during the early months of a puppy's development. If you do plan to show your Shih Tzu, what you hopefully will have acquired is a puppy with show "potential."

To the novice, exhibiting a Shih Tzu in the ring may look easy, but it takes a lot of hard work and devotion to win at a show such as the Westminster Kennel Club Dog Show, not to mention a little luck, too!

The first thing that the canine novice learns when watching a dog show is that each dog first competes against members of his own breed. Once the judge has selected the best member of each breed (Best of Breed) the chosen dog will compete with other dogs in its group. Finally, the dogs chosen first in each group will compete for Best in Show.

The second concept that you must understand is that the dogs are not compared against one another. The judge compares each dog against the breed standard, the written description of the ideal specimen approved by the AKC or UKC, depending on the sponsoring club. While some early breed standards were based on famous or popular dogs, many dedicated enthusiasts say that a perfect specimen as described in the standard has never walked into a show ring, has never been bred and, to the woe of dog breeders around the globe, does not exist. Breeders attempt to get as close to this ideal as possible with every litter, but theoretically the "perfect" dog is so elusive that it is impossible. (And if the perfect dog were born, breeders and judges probably would never agree that he was perfect.)

If you are interested in exploring the world of conformation, your best bet is to join your local breed club or the national (or parent) club, the American Shih Tzu Club. These clubs often host regional and national specialties, shows only for Shih Tzu, which can include conformation as well as obedience and field trials. Even if you have no intention of competing with your Shih Tzu, a specialty is a like a festival for lovers of the breed who congregate to share their favorite topic: Shih Tzu! Clubs also send out newsletters and some organize training days and seminars in order that people may learn more about their chosen breed.

THERAPY DOGS

Therapy work offers a special kind of satisfaction, the gratification of bringing pleasure simply through your dog's presence. If you like helping people, you and your Shih Tzu can bring happiness and laughter to people who are confined to hospitals and nursing homes. Therapy-dog visits are a wonderful way for you to share the joys of owning a Shih Tzu with others. Petting your dog can ease the loneliness of a widower in a nursing home, lower the blood pressure of a hospital patient and win big grins and laughs from children in a cancer ward.

Your therapy Shih Tzu must be clean, free of fleas and exhibit good manners. No

An event — aka a dog show — that lets Shih Tzu strut their stuff?! Count them in!

Sports are physically demanding. Have your vet do a full examination of your Shih Tzu to rule out joint problems, heart disease, eye ailments and other maladies. Once you get a health clearance, start having fun in your new dog-sporting life!

food stealing or potty accidents! He must pass a temperament test to ensure that he's suited for this type of work. A sweet, tolerant, fearless disposition is ideal because therapy work involves encounters with new or unusual places, people and equipment. Both of you will attend training classes before visits begin. Be sure to take normal precautions against falls from aged, shaky hands or run-ins with wheelchairs or walkers. A short leash attached to a harness will help you keep control.

CANINE GOOD CITIZEN

If obedience work sounds too regimented but you'd still like your Shih Tzu to have a title, prepare him for the Canine Good Citizen test. This program is sponsored by the AKC with tests administered by local dog clubs, private trainers and 4-H clubs.

To earn a CGC title, your Shih Tzu must be well-groomed and demonstrate the manners that all good dogs should exhibit. The CGC test requires a dog to perform the sit, down, stay, and come commands; react appropriately to other dogs and distractions; allow a stranger to approach him; sit politely for petting; walk nicely on a loose lead; move through a crowd without going wild; calm down after play or praise and sit still for examination by the judge. Rules are posted on www.akc.org, or find more information

at DogChannel.com/Club-Shih Tzu and click on downloads.

SMALL DOG SAFETY

Your Shih Tzu will probably be the smallest dog in your dog sport training class. Many dogs aren't familiar with toy breeds and react as if Shih Tzu are prey. An excited larger dog pouncing on your dog could cause serious injuries before anyone could intervene, so make sure that while your dog is running all larger dogs are securely held by their handlers, tethered to something immovable, or crated. When large dogs are off-leash, either crate your Shih Tzu or hold her in your arms.

You don't have to be conventional in your sport choice. Your Shih Tzu will be up for most anything, as long as he is with you. Boating, anyone?!

A Shih Tzu Bodybuilder? No Way!

Wanting a Shih Tzu playmate for her spayed female, Pebbles, as well as a new agility and obedience prospect, Pam Wilson of Virginia Beach, Va., purchased Bam-Bam. Happy to serve as Pebble's playmate, this red-and-white male Shih Tzu proved less enthusiastic about agility.

"We hit a roadblock at the weavepoles," she says. "It was apparent how much he disliked them."

Rather than push him to perform in a sport not to his taste, Wilson pulled Bam-Bam from agility competition. During this time, fate stepped in when a nearby United Kennel Club group started offering weight-pulling events.

"A few new members convinced me that even a Shih Tzu could pull the small cart," she recalls. "So they loaned me a harness used on one of their big dogs as a puppy. Bam-Bam wore the harness just like it was a sweater, and I hitched him up to the small, 80-pound cart. He pulled it without any problems. Then, we added a few small weights until he was pulling 100 pounds."

Then, Wilson decided to see how far Bam-Bam could go in this new activity. Soon fitted with a handmade harness boasting "Shih Tzu Power" on the side, Bam-Bam was ready to work. However, strength training differed for Bam-Bam in comparison to his weight-pulling companions. "Experienced competitors suggest having the dog drag a car tire to build strength," Wilson explains. Knowing that might be a bit much for her 13-pound mighty mite, she loaded a laundry basket full of dirty clothes and had him pull it down a carpeted hallway.

At his next event, Bam-Bam pulled nearly 200 pounds! With additional training and experience, this amazing little dog pulled a whopping 592 pounds on carpet with a wheeled cart. "That would be about 42 times his body weight," Wilson proudly points out.

What motivates him do it?

"He really understands he needs to come to me at the end of the chute, despite pulling something behind him that weighs so much more than he does," Wilson says. "It has been said that Shih Tzu comes from a Chinese word for 'lion dog.' Well, this dog has the heart of a lion, because he proves it over and over each time he pulls."

If you think your own little lion might enjoy this sport, contact local training clubs to ask if any members actively pursue weight pulling. Also, check with UKC clubs or large-breed clubs, such as Alaskan Malamute, Samoyed and other draft-type dogs. You can also contact the International Weight Pull Association. You never know, your Shih Tzu may find her calling and follow in Bam-Bam's footsteps.

Y ou can find out more information about Shih Tzu by contacting the following organizations.

American Kennel Club: The AKC website offers information and links to conformation, rally, obedience and agility programs and member clubs. www.akc.org

American Shih Tzu Club: This is the AKC–recognized breed club. The site includes health, grooming and contact information. www.americanshihtzuclub.org

Association of Pet Dog Trainers: If you are looking for a great trainer, start here. www.apdt.com

Canadian Kennel Club: Our northern neighbor's oldest kennel club is similar to the AKC. www.ckc.ca

Love on a Leash: There are more than 900 members of this pet therapy organization. www.loveonaleash.org

North American Dog Agility Council: This site provides links to clubs, events and agility trainers in the United States and Canada. www.nadac.com

North American Flyball Association: This growing-in-popularity dog sport combines racing, tennis-ball fetching and fun. Each team of four dogs needs small members to set the jump heights. www.flyball.org

it's a **Fact**

The **American Kennel Club** was started in 1884. It is America's oldest kennel club. The **United Kennel Club** is the second oldest in the United States. It began registering dogs in 1898.

Therapy Dogs Inc.: Get you and your Shih Tzu involved in helping others with therapy training. www.therapydogs.com

Therapy Dogs International: Find more therapy dog info here: www.tdi-dog.org

United Kennel Club: The UKC offers many events offered by the AKC, including agility, conformation and obedience. The UKC also offers junior programs. www.ukc dogs.com

United States Dog Agility Association: The USDAA has information on agility training, local clubs and local and national events in the United States, Canada, Mexico and overseas: www.usdaa.com

World Canine Freestyle Organization: With some fancy training, clever costumes and a catchy tune, you'll be dancing with your dog in no time. www.worldcanine freestyle.org

BOARDING

So you want to take a family vacation, and you want to include all members of the family. You usually make arrangements ahead of time anyway, but this is imperative when traveling with a Shih Tzu. You do not want to make an overnight stop at the only place around for miles and find out the hotel doesn't allow dogs. Also, you do not want to reserve a room for your family without confirming that you are traveling with a dog, because if it is against the hotel's policy, you may not have a place to stay.

Alternatively, if you are traveling and choose not to bring your Shih Tzu, you will have to make arrangements for him. Some options are to bring him to a family member or a neighbor, have a trusted friend stop by often, stay at your house or bring your dog to a reputable boarding kennel.

If you choose to board him at a kennel, visit in advance to see the facilities and check how clean they are and where the dogs are kept. Talk to some of the employees and see how they treat the dogs; do they spend time with the dogs, play with them, exercise them, etc.? Also, find out the kennel's policy on vaccinations and what they require. This is for all of the dogs' safety because when dogs are kept together, there is a greater risk of diseases being passed from dog to dog.

HOME STAFFING

For the Shih Tzu owner who works during the day or finds himself away from home on certain days, a pet sitter or dog walker may be the perfect solution for a lonely Shih Tzu who longs for a midday stroll and a romp at the dog park. Smart dog owners can approach local high schools or community centers if they can't find a neighbor interested in a part-time commitment. Interview potential dog walkers and consider their experience with dogs and your Shih Tzu's rapport with the candidate. (Shih Tzu are excellent judges of character!) Always check references before entrusting your Shih Tzu as well as your home to a new dog walker.

For an owner's long-term absence, such as a business trip or vacation, many Shih Tzu owners welcome the services of a pet sitter. It's usually less stressful for your dog to stay home with a pet sitter than to be boarded in a kennel. Pet sitters also may be more affordable than a week's stay at a full-service doggie day care.

Don't get so caught up in your excitement to go on vacation that you forget to make arrangements for your Shih Tzu.

Pet sitters must be more reliable than dog walkers because your Shih Tzu will be depending on him for all of his needs for an extended period. Smart owners are advised to hire a certified pet sitter through the National Association of Professional Pet Sitters. This nonprofit organization certifies professional individuals who are knowledgeable in canine behavior, nutrition, health and safety. A

Always keep your Shih Tzu's best interest at heart when planning a trip!

SCHOOL'S IN SESSION

Puppy kindergarten, which is usually open to puppies between 3 to 6 months, allows puppies to learn and socialize with other dogs and people in a structured setting. Classes help your Shih Tzu enjoy going places with you and help your dog become a well-behaved member at public gatherings that include other dogs. They prepare him for adult obedience classes, as well as for life.

The problem with most puppy kindergarten classes is that most are held only one night a week. What about during the rest of the week? If you're at home all week, you may be able to find other places to take your puppy, but you have to be careful about dog parks and other places where just any dog can go. An experience with a bully can undo all the good your classes have done, or worse, end in tragedy.

If you work, your puppy may be home alone all day, a tough situation for a Shih Tzu. Chances are he can't hold his urine in for that long, so your potty training will be undermined unless you're just aiming to teach him to use an indoor potty. And chances are, by the time you come home, he'll be bursting with energy, and you may start to think he's hyperactive.

The answer for the professional with a Shih Tzu is doggie day care. Most larger cities have some sort of day care, whether it's a boarding kennel that keeps your dog in a run or a full-service day care that offers training, play time and even spa facilities. They range from a person who keeps a few dogs at his home to a state-of-the-art facility just for dogs. Many of the more sophisticated doggie day cares offer webcams so you can see your dog throughout the day. Here are some things to look for:

- escape-proof facilities
- inoculation requirements for new dogs
- midday meals for young dogs
- obedience training using reward-based methods
- safe and comfortable sleep areas
- screening dogs for aggression
- small groups of similar sizes and ages
- toys and playground equipment
- trained staff, with an adequate number to supervise the dogs (no more than 10 to 15 dogs per person)
- a webcam

SMART TIP!

Remember to keep your Shih Tzu's leash slack when interacting with other dogs. It is not unusual for a toy dog to pick out one or two canine neighbors to dislike. If you know there's bad blood, step off to the side and put a barrier, such as a parked car, between the dogs. If there are no barriers to be had, move to the side of the walkway, cue your dog to sit, stay and watch you until her nemesis passes; then continue your walk.

CAR TRAVEL

You should acclimate your Shih Tzu to riding in a car at an early age. You may or may not plan to take him in the car often, but who are we kidding? Of course, you will! At the very least, he will need to go to the vet, and you do not want these trips to be traumatize your dog or be troublesome for you. The safest way for your dog to ride in the car is in his crate. If he uses a crate in the house, you can use the same crate for travel.

Another option for your portable dog is a specially made safety harness for dogs, which straps him in the car, much like a seat belt. Do not let your dog roam loose in the vehicle or ride in your lap: This is very dangerous! If you should stop abruptly, your dog can be thrown and injured. If your dog starts climbing on you and pestering you while you are driving, you will not be able to concentrate on the road. It is an unsafe situation for everyone — human and canine alike.

For long trips, stop often to let your Shih Tzu relieve himself. Pack items to clean up after him, including some paper towels should he have an accident in the car or suffer from motion sickness.

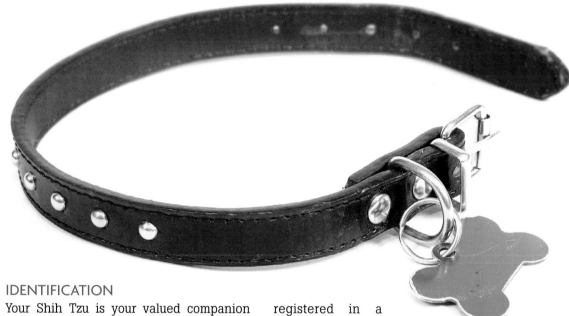

IDENTIFICATION

Your Shih Tzu is your valued companion and friend. That is why you always keep a close eye on him and you have made sure that he cannot escape from the yard or wriggle out of his collar and run away. However, accidents can happen and there may come a time when your dog unexpectedly gets separated from you. If this should occur, the first thing on your mind will be finding him. Proper identification, including an ID tag, a tattoo and possibly a microchip will increase the chances of his being returned to you safely and quickly.

An ID tag on a collar or harness is the primary means of pet identification (ID licenses are required in many communities). Although inexpensive and easy to read, collars and ID tags can come off or be removed too easily.

A microchip doesn't get lost. Containing a unique ID number that can be read by scanners, the microchip is embedded underneath a dog's skin. It's invaluable for identifying lost or stolen pets. However, in order to be effective, the microchip must be registered in a nationwide database.

Smart owners will constantly make sure their contact information is kept up-to-date. Additionally, not every shelter or veterinary clinic has a scanner, nor do most folks who try to return a lost dog to his owner.

Your best bet is to get both!

Did You Know?

Some communities have created regular dog runs and separate spaces for small dogs. These dog runs are ideal for introducing puppies to the dog park experience. The runs and participants are smaller and their owners are often more vigilant because they are used to watching out for their fragile companions.

INDEX

SHIH TZU, a Smart Owner's Guide®

LIBRARY OF CONGRESS CATALOGING-IN-PUBLICATION DATA

Shih tzu / from the editors of Dog fancy magazine.
    p. cm. — (Smart owner's guide)
Includes bibliographical references and index.
ISBN 978-1-59378-749-3
1. Shih tzu. I. Dog fancy (San Juan Capistrano, Calif.)
SF429.S64S55 2010
636.76—dc22

                2009029023

JOIN Club Shih Tzu® TODAY!